CPE Practice Tests 2

Virginia Evans – Jenny Dooley

Student's Book

Express Publishing

Published by Express Publishing

Liberty House, Greenham Business Park, Newbury, Berkshire RG19 6HW, United Kingdom
Tel: (0044) 1635 817 363 - Fax: (0044) 1635 817 463
email: inquiries@expresspublishing.co.uk
www.expresspublishing.co.uk

© Virginia Evans – Jenny Dooley, 2013

Design and Illustration © Express Publishing, 2013

First published in this edition 2013
Third impression 2016

Made in EU

ISBN 978-1-4715-0758-8

Acknowledgements

The authors and publishers also wish to thank the following for their kind permission to use copyright material: *"Can I kick it? Yes you cancan"*, by Philip French, © The Observer, for the excerpt-adapted on p. 6; *"Jung"*, by Robert Matthews, © Focus, on p. 8; *"Survival of the most stubborn"*, by Paula Kahumbu, © The Guardian, on p. 12; Extract from *"The Age of Innocence"*, by Edith Wharton, © 1994, Wordsworth Editions Limited, on pp. 14-15; Flashback *"Skeleton Crew"*, by Patricia Zackowitz © National Geographic, March 1999/*"On Assignment"*, by Patricia Zackowitz © National Geographic, March 1999, on p. 17; *"Witch to Saint – The lady who spent 50 years alone in the desert"*, © Focus, on p. 17; *"Egypt's hidden tombs"*, by Zahi Hawass, © National Geographic, Sept 2001, on p. 17; *"Zoos"*, by Nigel Hicks, © Focus, on p. 18; Extract from *"The Cambridge Encyclopedia of the English Language"*, by David Crystal, 1995. © Cambridge University Press, on p. 22; *"Send in the clowns"* by Anita Chaudhuri, © The Guardian, on p. 23; *"We deal in lead my friend"*, © Focus, on p. 26; *"Pretend to be brainy"*, by Catherine Zandonella, © New Scientist RBI Ltd, 28/4/2001, on p. 28; *"El Nino - La Nina"*, by Curt Suplee, National Geographic, March 1999, on p. 29; *"Marco Polo"*, by Patricia Kellogg, © National Geographic, www.national geographic.com/ngm/0105/feature1/index.html, on p. 32; *"It'll be ok on the day"*, by Tracy Hawthorne, © FAIRLADY/Media24, on p. 37; *"A feast of colour and ceremony"*, by Pricilla Singh, © FAIRLADY/Media24, on p. 37; *"Work. Fighting off the techno invader"*, by Nick Gillies, on p. 38. Thanks to Nick Gillies, who is a London-based freelance journalist, who writes about the work and management of the professions; *"Ergonomics Concepts"* © 2002, Ergoweb Inc. Used by permission.www.ergoweb.com, on p. 38; New Moon, March,"Set up a bird feeding station"/"Find a local patch..." © BBC Wildlife, March 1997, on p. 40; *"Making a difference"*, © Polly Ghazi /BBC Wildlife, on p. 42; *"World Champions in the making"*, © Focus, on p. 43; *"The World's bankers: The Rothschilds"*, © Focus, on p. 46; *"What the eye didn't see"*, © Andrew Marr, The Observer, on p. 52; *"Cuba's Golden Past"*, by Tom Allen. © National Geographic. July 2001, on pp. 54-55; *"Colour Blindness"*, Microsoft ® Encarta ® Encyclopedia. http://encarta.msn.com ©1993-2001 Microsoft Corporation. All rights reserved, on p. 60; *"Jumping Great Whites"*, by Gaia Vince, © Focus, on p. 62; *"Class Struggles"*, by Nick Cohen, © The Observer, on p. 72; *"Spellbound"*, by Allan Coukell, © New Scientist, RBI Ltd, 19/5/2001, on pp. 74-75; *"American travels of a gem collector, part 1"*, by George F Kuntz. Text reproduced courtesy of Richard Hughes/RWH Publishing & Books, on p. 77; *"Burmese Jade: The inscrutable Gem - part 1: Burma's Jade Mines"*, by R Hughes, O G Bosshart, F Ward, T Te Sun, T Oo, G E. Harlow. Text reproduced courtesy of Richard Hughes/RWH Publishing & Books, on p. 77; *"A dyslexic child in the classroom, a guide for teachers and parents"*, © Patricia Hodge, on p. 78; *"The Great Fire of London"*, Thanks to Elizabeth Batt, link: www.adastrapublishing.com, on p. 80; *"Gold"*, © Focus, on p. 86; *"A plague on all your houses"*, by Jonathan Glancey, © The Guardian, on p. 88; *"Charles Booth's London"*, forward by Raymond Williams, © Raymond Williams. Used by permission of The Random House Group Limited, on pp. 94-95; *"100 years of gadgets"*, by Caroline Elliot, © Focus, on p. 97; *"Egypt yields up its sunken treasures"*, by Brian Whitaker, © The Guardian, on p. 101; *"Missile Technology Ensures Fair Play"*, © Focus, on p. 106; *"The world keeps turning and tilting, but autumn's clock runs slower"*, by Paul Evans, © The Guardian, on p. 108; Extract from "Monosodium glutamate: Dispelling the myths", Australian Glutamate Information Service. website: www.msg.org.au, on p. 117; *"Green Acres"*, by Rob Mahoney, Sept 1998 issue of Prepared Foods. website: www. PreparedFoods.com, on p. 117; *"Chillisgalore"*, reproduced with the permission of Kathy Thompson, www.chillisgalore.co.uk, on p. 117; *"The tortoise and the hairpin"*, by Mark Cocker, © The Guardian, on p. 120; *"Excavate dinosaur fossils in the Gobi"*, © Nomadic Expeditions, on p. 123; Special thanks to Britannica Macropaedia.

Every effort has been made to trace all the copyright holders. If any have been inadvertently overlooked, the publishers will be pleased to make the necessary arrangements at the first opportunity.

Contents

Introduction

CPE Practice Tests 2 contains six complete tests designed to help students to prepare for the University of Cambridge Local Examinations Syndicate (UCLES) Certificate of Proficiency in English (CPE) examination. The tests offer comprehensive practice in all four papers of the examination and reflect the revised exam which will be introduced from March 2013, thus providing students with the tools to develop the skills required to succeed in this examination and obtain the CPE qualification.

CPE Practice Tests 2 includes a wide range of stimulating, authentic texts in examination format, listening texts with authenticated recordings and a variety of accents, and full-colour visual material for the Speaking Test.

The *Student's Book* provides a detailed overview of the CPE examination, with a description of all the sections of each paper. It also provides exam guidance sections and guidelines on assessing and marking each paper.

The *Key* contains answers to all the exercises in the *Student's Book*, model written answers for Paper 2 – Writing, tapescripts of the recorded material for the Listening paper, and guidelines for the Speaking Test.

About CPE

CPE is at the fifth level in the UCLES five-level series of examinations and is designed to offer an advanced qualification, suitable for those who want to use English for professional or academic study purposes. At this level, the learner is approaching the linguistic competence of an educated native speaker and is able to use the language in a wide range of culturally appropriate ways. CPE is recognised by the majority of British universities for English language entrance requirements. It is also widely recognised throughout the world by universities, institutes of higher education, professional bodies as well as in commerce and industry as an indication of a very high level of competence in English.

Cambridge Level Five Certificate of Proficiency in English (CPE)
Cambridge Level Four Certificate in Advanced English (CAE)
Cambridge Level Three First Certificate in English (FCE)
Cambridge Level Two Preliminary English Test (PET)
Cambridge Level One Key English Test (KET)

In CPE there are **four** Papers as shown below:

Paper 1	*(1 hour 30 mins)*		
Reading & Use of English	7 parts		

Paper 2	*(1 hour 30 mins)*		
Writing	2 parts		

Paper 3	*(approximately 40 mins)*		
Listening	4 parts		

Paper 4	*(16 mins)*		
Speaking	3 parts		

PAPER 1

READING & USE OF ENGLISH   (1 hour 30 mins)
This paper has 7 parts with 53 questions drawn from texts with between 2,900-3,400 words in total.

Part 1
A modified cloze containing eight gaps followed by eight 4-option multiple-choice items.
Test focus: idioms, collocations, fixed phrases, complementation, phrasal verbs and semantic precision.   *(1 mark per question)*

Part 2
A modified cloze test containing eight gaps.
Task focus: awareness and control of grammar with some focus on vocabulary.   *(1 mark per question)*

Part 3
A text containing eight gaps each of which corresponds to a word. The stem of the word is given beside the text and must be changed to form the missing word.
Task focus: vocabulary, in particular the use of affixation, internal changes and compounding in word formation.
          (1 mark per question)

Part 4
Six items, each containing a lead-in sentence followed by a gapped second sentence to be completed with between 3 and 8 words. The sentences must contain the given 'key' word.
Task focus: grammar, vocabulary and collocation.
          (2 marks per question)

Part 5
A text followed by six four-option multiple-choice questions.
Task focus: detail, opinion, attitude, tone, purpose, main idea, implication and text organisation features (exemplification, reference).   *(2 marks per question)*

Part 6
A text with seven paragraphs removed and placed in jumbled order after the text with one extra paragraph as a distractor.
Task focus: cohesion, coherence, text structure and global meaning.   *(2 marks per question)*

Part 7
A text or several short texts with ten multiple-matching questions whereby a prompt is matched to elements in the text.
Task focus: detail, opinion, attitude and specific information.
          (1 mark per question)
          (Total 72 marks)

PAPER 2

WRITING   (1 hour 30 mins)
This paper has two parts. Each question in this paper carries equal marks.

Part 1
A compulsory essay writing task of 240-280 words. The essay must summarise and evaluate the key ideas contained in two texts of approximately 100 words each. The texts may have complementary or contrasting opinions. They may also be extracts from newspapers, books, magazines, online source material or based on quotations from speakers in a discussion.
Task focus: a discursive essay.

Part 2
One task of 280-320 words from a choice of four. Questions 2-4 are tasks with a clear context, topic, purpose and target reader. Question 5 is a choice between two tasks based on the set reading texts.

Task types: essay, report, article, letter and review.
Task focus: writing one of the tasks from a number of possible text types based on either a contextualised writing task or a question related to one of two set texts.

PAPER 3

LISTENING   (approximately 40 minutes)
This paper has four parts, each containing a recorded text/texts with corresponding comprehension tasks. Each part is heard twice.

Part 1
Three short texts of approx. 1 minute each, consisting of either monologues or dialogues with two multiple-choice questions for each extract.
Task focus: identifying feeling, attitude, opinion, purpose, agreement between speakers, course of action, gist and detail.
          (1 mark per question)

Part 2
A monologue of 3-4 mins with 9 sentence completion questions.
Task focus: identifying specific information and stated opinion.
          (1 mark per question)

Part 3
An interview or conversation between two or more speakers of approx. 4 minutes with five 4-option multiple-choice questions.
Task focus: identifying attitude, opinion, gist, detail and inference.   *(1 mark per question)*

Part 4
Five short, themed monologues of approx. 30 seconds each with two tasks, each containing five questions requiring the selection of the correct option from a list of eight.
Task focus: identifying gist, attitude, main points and interpreting context.   *(1 mark per question)*
          (Total 30)

PAPER 4

SPEAKING   (approximately 16 minutes)
This paper contains three parts and is taken by the candidates in pairs with two examiners present. One of the examiners acts as interlocutor and the other one as assessor.

Part 1
Conversation between the interlocutor and each candidate. The interlocutor encourages candidates to give information about themselves and express personal opinions.
Task focus: using general interactional and social language.

Part 2
Two-way conversation between the candidates based on written and visual prompts.
Task focus: sustaining an interaction, exchanging ideas, expressing/justifying opinions, agreeing/disagreeing, suggesting, speculating, evaluating, reaching decisions through negotiation etc.

Part 3
Individual long turn by each candidate followed by a discussion on topics related to the long turn. Each candidate is given a written question to respond to. The candidates then engage in a discussion to explore further the long turn topics.
Task focus: organising a larger unit of discourse, expressing/justifying opinions and developing topics.

PRACTICE TEST 1

Paper 1 – Reading & Use of English *(1 hour 30 minutes)*

Part 1

For questions **1-8**, read the text below and decide which answer (**A**, **B**, **C** or **D**) best fits each gap. Mark your answers **on the separate answer sheet**.

There is an example at the beginning **(0)**.

0 **A** appropriated **B** captured **C** annexed **D** mastered

0	A	B	C	D
	☐	■	☐	☐

Australian Cinema

Thirty years ago, the New Australian cinema **(0)** ....B.... the attention of the world with heroic stories set in the late-nineteenth and early-twentieth centuries. They were tales of the formation of a national **(1)** ...., of the recent settlers transactions with their strange new world and its frighteningly mystical inhabitants. When this vein was **(2)** ...., local film makers left home or turned to the problematic present of people living lives of noisy desperation in the **(3)** .... suburbs of the big coastal cities, home to most Australians. As television series, these cosy, unheroic stories **(4)** .... worldwide popularity, but relatively few films of this sort have found success elsewhere, except for a small **(5)** .... among which are these **(6)** .... accomplished and calculatedly theatrical films. They are loving assemblages of **(7)** .... and cliches from the musicals of the past, produced with an exuberance that **(8)** .... the audience up in uncritical enjoyment.

1	A	personality	B	unity	C	identity	D	parity
2	A	exhausted	B	drained	C	emptied	D	squandered
3	A	lounging	B	stooping	C	stretching	D	sprawling
4	A	reached	B	achieved	C	fulfilled	D	managed
5	A	dusting	B	handful	C	few	D	bit
6	A	deeply	B	heavily	C	highly	D	widely
7	A	conventions	B	mores	C	protocols	D	manners
8	A	sweeps	B	cleans	C	brushes	D	carries

Part 2

For questions **9-16**, read the text below and think of the word which best fits each space. Use only **one** word in each space. There is an example at the beginning (**0**). Write your answers **IN CAPITAL LETTERS on the separate answer sheet**.

Example: | 0 | F | A | R | | | | | | | | | | | | | | | | |

AN INFLUENTIAL MAN

Born in Switzerland in 1875, Carl Gustav Jung's early life was (**0**) ......FAR..... from conventional. The (**9**) .... child of a country pastor with waning religious convictions and a spiritualist mother (**10**) .... conversed with ghosts, Jung felt alienated and lonely as a child. He spent his life trying to understand the nature of the human psyche, to probe the human mind to see what lurked beneath. (**11**) .... he found helped form the foundations of modern psychology, identifying such familiar concepts as introversion and extroversion as (**12**) .... as complexes. Jung went (**13**) .... than the mainstream of science. He delved into ancient myths and religions and the esoteric literature of alchemy and astrology. (**14**) .... his research, he discovered recurrent images that he argued revealed the existence of a 'collective unconscious' we all share. Such findings have made his work influential in fields well (**15**) .... psychology, permeating literature, religion and culture.

Today Jungian analysis attracts a steady stream of patients seeking solace from the personal difficulties in their lives. With more people than (**16**) .... discovering that 'success' often fails to bring happiness, the importance of Jung's efforts to find contentment have never been clearer.

Part 3

For questions **17-24**, read the text below. Use the word given in capitals at the end of some of the lines to form a word that fits in the space in the same line. There is an example at the beginning (**0**). Write your answers **IN CAPITAL LETTERS on the separate answer sheet**.

Example: | **0** | E | S | T | A | B | L | I | S | H | M | E | N | T | | | | | |

Coffee

Today's café is a small eating and drinking **(0)** .......ESTABLISHMENT......., yet, **ESTABLISH**

(17) .... it was a coffee house which served only coffee. The **HISTORY**

English term, café, borrowed from the French, is ultimately a

(18) .... of the Turkish kahve, meaning coffee. The **DERIVE**

introduction of coffee and coffee drinking to Europe provided a much needed

focus for the social **(19)** .... of the middle classes. The first **ACT**

café is said to have opened in Constantinople in 1550. By the end of the 17th

century coffee houses had opened across Europe. From the mid 17th century

and for the next 200 years the most **(20)** .... in Europe were the **PROSPER**

coffee houses of London. These flourished as meeting points for endless

discussions of the latest news, indulging in raucous **(21)** .... **AGREE**

and for the **(22)** .... business of buying and selling **LUCRE**

insurance ships, stocks and commodities. They were also informal stations for

the collection and distribution of packets and letters. At about the same time,

the French café was at its zenith as a gathering place for artists and

(23) .... and it continued to be an important social **INTELLECT**

institution in France throughout the 20th century. Nowadays, with the rise in

popularity of different types of coffee, such as espresso and latte, large

numbers of outlets **(24)** .... in coffee have opened. **SPECIAL**

9

Part 4

For questions **25-30**, complete the second sentence so that it has a similar meaning to the first sentence, using the word given. **Do not change the word given.** You must use between **three** and **eight** words, including the word given. Here is an example (**0**).

Example:

0   Louise should have been given more time to complete her thesis.

   insufficient

   Louise .... thesis.

| 0 | *was given insufficient time to complete her* |

Write **only** the missing words **on the separate answer sheet**.

---

25   We have to think carefully about our other expenses before we decide to buy a new car.

   taken

   Our other expenses .... before we decide to buy a new car.

26   She believed she was very likely to win the scholarship.

   chance

   She believed .... the scholarship.

27   Yesterday, I seemed to do nothing but answer the phone.

spend

Yesterday, I seemed .... the phone.

28   It seems that Amy was offended by what you said.

offence

Amy .... what you said.

29   We are unlikely to have nice weather for our picnic tomorrow.

prospect

There is .... for our picnic tomorrow.

30   We are able to afford a holiday as I was promoted.

result

As ...., we are able to afford a holiday.

Part 5

You are going to read an extract which discusses the work of a famous conservationist. For questions **31-36**, choose the answer (**A, B, C** or **D**) which you think fits best according to the text. Mark your answers **on the separate answer sheet**.

Leakey's Achievement

Although he made his name with his archaeological finds of early humans, Richard Leakey became famous as the conservationist who turned the tide against elephant poaching. Bringing the slaughter of Kenya's elephants under control required a military solution, and Leakey was not afraid to apply it. Many poachers were killed, giving Leakey a reputation for being a cold-blooded obsessive who put animals before people. Moreover, his efforts to eradicate corruption in Kenya's wildlife management system won him many enemies.

But the birth of the Kenya Wildlife Service (KWS), the eradication of elephant poaching and the ban on the international trade in ivory are his legacy, and they form the basis of *Wildlife Wars*. This surprisingly personal memoir has much to tell about the fragile relationships between conservationists and governments. It is a story not only of Kenya, but of the continuing cost of trying to save the world's wildlife from extinction.

Life for the average person in Africa is tough, and basic needs are far from being met. This is the background against which Leakey fought his war, and he constantly refers to the threat poverty poses to the preservation of Africa's spectacular wildlife. Leakey's argument, here and in recent lectures, is that national parks managed exclusively for biodiversity protection must be created, and that this protection of our wildlife heritage should be funded by international sources.

However, in the early 1990s the development agencies favoured "community-based" conservation. Leakey's stand on the protection of parks was seen as a lack of respect for local communities, and used against him when he resigned as head of the KWS in 1994. Recently donors and conservationists have come to recognise the limitations of purely local conservation programmes; there is a growing consensus that the poor are unlikely to manage wildlife resources wisely for the long term because their needs are immediate.

Wildlife Wars continues where Leakey's memoir *One Life* left off. It spans a 13-year period, beginning in 1989 when Leakey became head of the KWS. Then the elephant slaughter was at its height across Africa; it is estimated that between 1975 and 1989 the international markets for ivory in Europe, the United States and Asia led to the death of 1.2 m elephants, slaughtered for their ivory to make piano keys, games and fashion accessories. Kenya's herds were reduced by more than 85% by armed poachers, who turned their guns on anything and anyone. To stop this killing required changing the perceptions of ivory users so as to eliminate the markets, as well as mounting an armed force against the poachers.

With both humour and seriousness, Leakey explains the sacrifices he had to make in order to see his vision succeed. Despite the gravity of the situation, Leakey makes light of the sometimes comical circumstances, although it is clear that his life was at risk many times and he worked under tremendous pressure. For many, however, the real question is why this palaeoanthropologist should risk his life for wildlife. The answer may lie in Leakey's own depiction of himself, although obviously aggressive and driven while running KWS, as essentially reflective. Presenting in moving terms his introduction to elephant emotions and society, he describes his outrage at the moral and ethical implications of poaching and culling for ivory, arguing that elephants, apes, whales and dolphins have emotions so like those of humans that they deserve to be treated as such.

Hard-core wildlife groups sniggered at his 'bunny-hugging' tendencies, but they underestimated his impact. It is impossible to put a value on Leakey's work during those years. As the elephant population began to recover, Kenya's tourist industry revived to become the country's main source of revenue. An international awareness campaign centred on an ivory bonfire, which led to the ban on ivory trade and the collapse of ivory prices.

31 Richard Leakey is best known for

   A   increasing wildlife budgets.

   B   successfully stopping illegal hunting.

   C   removing the ban on the ivory trade.

   D   helping to identify man's origins.

32 In paragraph 3, Leakey makes the point that

   A   conservation should be a global responsibility.

   B   a war must be fought against poverty.

   C   Africa's wildlife is an international attraction.

   D   there is insufficient money to establish parks.

33 It is now becoming accepted that

   A   Leakey had no regard for local communities.

   B   conservation programmes should be under local control.

   C   donors have not yet received sufficient recognition.

   D   poverty makes regional conservation programmes unreliable.

34 The writer says that between 1975 and 1989

   A   the perceptions of the use of ivory changed.

   B   elephants were used to make piano keys.

   C   the elephant population was decimated.

   D   demand for ivory began to decrease.

35 What does the writer imply in the last paragraph?

   A   A disease had affected elephants.

   B   Leakey's views are overly sentimental.

   C   Leakey's success is in doubt.

   D   Leakey's work had wide-ranging effects.

36 This passage is taken from

   A   an article about endangered species.

   B   a book about Richard Leakey.

   C   an article about Kenya.

   D   a book review.

Part 6

You are going to read an extract from a novel. Seven paragraphs have been removed from the extract. Choose from the paragraphs **A-H** the one which fits each gap (**37-43**). There is one extra paragraph which you do not need to use. **Mark your answers on the separate answer sheet.**

Summer

The small, bright lawn stretched away smoothly to the big, bright sea. The turf was hemmed with an edge of scarlet geranium and coleus, and cast-iron vases painted in a chocolate colour, standing at intervals along the winding path that led to the sea, looped their garlands of petunia and ivy geranium above the neatly raked gravel.

37

A number of ladies in summer dresses and gentlemen in grey frock-coats and tall hats stood on the lawn or sat upon the benches. Every now and then, a slender girl in starched muslin would step from the tent, bow in hand, and speed her shaft at one of the targets, while the spectators interrupted their talk to watch the result.

38

The Newbury Archery Club always held its August meeting at the Beauforts'. The sport, which had hitherto known no rival but croquet, was beginning to be discarded in favour of lawn-tennis. However, the latter game was still considered too rough and inelegant for social occasions, and as an opportunity to show off pretty dresses and graceful attitudes, the bow and arrow held their own.

39

In New York, during the previous winter, after he and May had settled down in the new, greenish-yellow house with the bow-window and the Pompeian vestibule, he had dropped back with relief into the old routine of the office. The renewal of his daily activities had served as a link with his former self.

40

At the Century, he had found Winsett again, and at the Knickerbocker, the fashionable young men of his own set. And what with hours dedicated to the law and those given to dining out or entertaining friends at home, with an occasional evening at the opera or the theatre, the life he was living had still seemed a fairly real and inevitable sort of business.

41

But the Wellands always went to Newport, where they owned one of the square boxes on the cliffs, and their son-in-law could adduce no good reason why he and May should not join them there. As Mrs. Welland rather tartly pointed out, it was hardly worthwhile for May to have worn herself out trying on summer clothes in Paris, if she was not to be allowed to wear them; and this argument was of a kind to which Archer had as yet found no answer.

42

It was not May's fault, poor dear. If, now and then, during their travels, they had fallen slightly out of step, harmony had been restored by their return to conditions she was used to. He had always foreseen that she would not disappoint him; and he had been right. No, the time and place had been perfect for his marriage.

43

He could not say that he had been mistaken in his choice, for she fulfilled all that he had expected. It was undoubtedly gratifying to be the husband of one of the handsomest and most popular young married women in New York, especially when she was also one of the sweetest-tempered and most reasonable of wives; and Archer had not been insensible to such advantages.

A   May herself could not understand his obscure reluctance to fall in with so reasonable and pleasant a way of spending the summer. She reminded him that he had always liked Newport in his bachelor days, and as this was indisputable, he could only profess that he was sure he was going to like it better than ever now that they were to be there together. But as he stood on the Beaufort verandah and looked out on the brightly peopled lawn, it came home to him with a shiver that he was not going to like it at all.

B   In addition, there had been the pleasurable excitement of choosing a showy grey horse for May's brougham (the Wellands had given the carriage). Then, there was the abiding occupation and interest of arranging his new library, which, in spite of family doubts and disapproval, had been carried out as he had dreamed, with a dark-embossed paper, an Eastlake book-case and "sincere" armchairs and tables.

C   The next morning Archer scoured the town in vain for more yellow roses. In consequence of this search, he arrived late at the office, perceived that his doing so made no difference whatever to anyone, and was filled with sudden exasperation at the elaborate futility of his life. Why should he not be, at that moment, on the sands of St. Augustine with May Welland?

D   Newland Archer, standing on the verandah of the Beaufort house, looked curiously down upon this scene. On each side of the shiny painted steps, was a large, blue china flowerpot on a bright yellow china stand. A spiky, green plant filled each pot, and below the verandah ran a wide border of blue hydrangeas edged with more red geraniums. Behind him, the French windows of the drawing rooms through which he had passed gave glimpses, between swaying lace curtains, of glassy parquet floors islanded with chintz pouffes, dwarf armchairs, and velvet tables covered with trifles of silver.

E   Archer looked down with wonder at the familiar spectacle. It surprised him that life should be going on in the old way when his own reactions to it had so completely changed. It was Newport that had first brought home to him the extent of the change.

F   Archer had married (as most young men did) because he had met a perfectly charming girl at the moment when a series of rather aimless sentimental adventures were ending in a premature disgust; and she had represented peace, stability, comradeship, and the steadying sense of an inescapable duty.

G   Half-way between the edge of the cliff and the square wooden house (which was also chocolate-coloured, but with the tin roof of the verandah striped in yellow and brown to represent an awning), two large targets had been placed against a background of shrubbery. On the other side of the lawn, facing the targets, was pitched a real tent, with benches and garden-seats about it.

H   Newport, on the other hand, represented the escape from duty into an atmosphere of unmitigated holiday-making. Archer had tried to persuade May to spend the summer on a remote island off the coast of Maine (called, appropriately enough, Mount Desert) where a few hardy Bostonians and Philadelphians were camping in native cottages, and whence came reports of enchanting scenery and a wild, almost trapper-like existence amid woods and waters.

Part 7

You are going to read four extracts which are all connected with exploration and discovery. For questions **44-53**, choose from the sections **(A-D)**. The sections may be chosen more than once.

Mark your answers **on the separate answer sheet**.

In which section are the following mentioned?

the extremely frugal lifestyle of a researcher	**44** ....
the problems associated with the continued preservation of a site	**45** ....
the availability of funds for particular types of researchers	**46** ....
an ability to navigate an area without technological help	**47** ....
a description of an ancient piece of sculpture	**48** ....
a summary of a region's historical culture	**49** ....
the suffering travellers endured on a journey	**50** ....
the promotion of interdisciplinary cooperation	**51** ....
the discovery of a lost monument	**52** ....
preventing the destruction of an ancient site	**53** ....

Exploration and Discovery

A Travelling Across the Desert

Crossing the Sahara is a dangerous business. George-Marie Haardt needed no reminder of this. During the desert leg of his 1924 expedition's 15,000 mile trip, the expedition's eight trucks travelled for 330 miles without finding a drop of water. 'Any breeze there is, becomes a torment,' the team reported. 'We are suffocated, saturated with dust; we could almost believe ourselves to be like men turned into red brick.' Writer Donovan Webster confirms this. 'People die all the time,' he says. 'That's why you go with someone you trust.' Don reckoned a little technology wouldn't hurt, though. 'When I mentioned to my guide, a Tuareg tribesman from Niger, that I had a GPS (global positioning system) receiver to help us navigate, he said he didn't need it,' says Don. 'I've got TPS,' he told me — 'Tuareg positioning system.' And he did! He could find his way anywhere just by seeing ripples in the sand. He was as interested in my world as I was in his,' Don recalls. 'When I showed him a photo of my kids at Niagara Falls, he wanted to keep it. He thought the kids were sweet — but couldn't imagine that much water in the world.'

B The Lady of the Lines

Maria Reiche, a German mathematician, devoted fifty years of her life to protecting and studying the Nazca lines of the Inca. Born in Dresden in 1903, she arrived in Peru, became fascinated by the Inca culture and initially found archaeological work. It was when, however, she overheard someone discussing giant figures carved into the ground south of Lima that she found what was to become her life's work. Instantly mesmerised by these strange objects, she began to study them alone. 'I walked along them to understand their meaning,' she said. 'I noticed that they formed figures, a spider, a monkey, a bird.' After surveying around 1,000 lines, she wrote her book *Mystery of the Desert,* published in 1949. In order to spend more time with the geoglyphs, she set up home on the edge of the desert, living off fruit and nuts and sleeping under the stars. If vandals dared to set foot near the lines, she shooed them away, so determined that the lines should be preserved that when plans were made to flood the area for agricultural use, she successfully blocked the move. Her tireless work has now resulted in the Nazca lines having been declared a World Heritage Site and she is regarded by some as a national heroine; she is Saint Maria, 'Lady of the Lines'. When she died in 1998 aged 95, the question arose of who would now protect the lines, which were becoming increasingly threatened by vandals, looters, irresponsible tourists and changing weather patterns. Fortunately, however, the UN's cultural agency has recently donated a substantial amount for their long-term conservation.

C Marine Research

The World Centre for Exploration has been running since 1904. Our international, professional society has been a meeting point and unifying force for explorers and scientists worldwide. The Explorers Club is dedicated to the advancement of field research, scientific exploration, and the ideal that it is vital to preserve the instinct to explore. We foster these goals by providing research grants, educational lectures and publications, expedition planning assistance, exciting adventure travel programmes, and a forum where experts in all the diverse fields of science and exploration can meet to exchange ideas. March will mark the fifth year of the running of the Kosa Reef Protection Project. The project is a joint effort by Kosa Marine resources, an international group of volunteer divers, and island support staff. Divers prepare fish inventories, photo and video records, and take scientific measurements documenting reef status. For the first time, this year's team will employ protocols developed by the international organisation 'Reef Check'. The Explorers Club also offers modest expedition grants for expeditions that forge links between space and earth exploration. Expeditions working in extreme environments or using satellite and space related technologies should contact us at the following address.

D Bahariya's Tombs

After 2,600 years, a desert oasis yields the long-sought tombs of its legendary governor and his family. The streets of El Bawiti, the largest town in Bahariya Oasis, are busier now. Hotels have been built since more than 200 Graeco-Roman mummies were discovered nearby. Yet, El Bawiti hid an older secret. The tombs of Bahariya's legendary governor, Zed-Khons-uef-ankh, his father, and his wife were discovered in a maze of chambers beneath local homes. Archaeologists had been looking for Zed-Khons-uef-ankh ever since the tombs of three of the governor's relatives were discovered in 1938. Zed-Khons-uef-ankh ruled Bahariya during Egypt's 26th dynasty, a time when the isolated oases of the Western Desert were strategically important buffers against invaders. Bahariya, with governors who were wealthy men with connections to the throne, flourished at the crossroads of caravan routes. Zed-Khons-uef-ankh, a man whose power to move men and material is most evident in the two mammoth stone sarcophagi that were transported across miles of sand and wasteland to his oasis tomb, had a chapel built in a temple nearby, with a relief depicting him as large as the pharaoh, a bold assertion from a powerful man we now know better.

Paper 2 – Writing *(1 hour 30 mins)*

Part 1

Read the two texts below.

Write an essay summarising and evaluating the key points from both texts. Use your own words throughout as far as possible, and include your own ideas in your answers.

Write your answer in **240-280 words on the separate answer sheet**.

1
Zoological Revolution

The role of the zoo has undergone a dramatic shift. The growing recognition that zoos ought to be in the vanguard of the fight against the devastation of our natural world began in the 1960s when Jersey Zoo was set up to breed endangered species. As a result, the breeding of animals in captivity is now a complex science, with zoos around the world coordinating their efforts to avoid the genetic dangers of inbreeding in small populations. Nonetheless, the impact of captive breeding programmes on the outlook for endangered species is probably minimal.

Changing Zoos

Zoos today are re-evaluating their purpose following growing awareness of the need for a greater role in conservation. This role generally involves the captive breeding of endangered species but, owing to the rapid disappearance of wild habitats, there is little hope for a widespread release of these animals, only that the existing stock of endangered species may be maintained. Many would argue that, because of the cost and limited impact of captive breeding, zoos should drop their breeding programmes and focus on protecting animals in their wild habitats. Thankfully, in-situ habitat protection is becoming a major part of the work of many zoos.

Write your **essay**.

Part 2

Write an answer to **one** of the questions **2-4** in this part. Write your answer in **280-320** words in an appropriate style **on the separate answer sheet**. Put the question number in the box at the top of the answer sheet.

2   A national TV channel has just begun the broadcast of a new reality TV show. You have been asked to write a review of the show for a local magazine. Write a review and say why these shows are so popular with some people and very unpopular with others.

   Write your **review**.

3   Your local town council has recently upgraded the town centre, including the building of a new shopping centre, pedestrianising the town centre streets and improving transport links from outlying areas. The council have invited reports from local people on the improvements. In your report comment on improvements made and whether they will have a positive or negative effect on the lives of local people.

   Write your **report**.

4   A business magazine has invited readers to contribute an article entitled *Why It's Good To Be Your Own Boss*. Write an article describing what kind of company you would like to set up and the advantages and disadvantages of running your own business.

   Write your **article**.

Paper 3 – Listening *(approx. 40 minutes)*

Part 1

You will hear three different extracts. For questions **1-6**, choose the answer (**A**, **B** or **C**) which fits best according to what you hear. There are two questions for each extract.

Extract One

You hear a gardening expert talking about her latest project.

1   What does the expert say about foliage plants?

    A   They are very versatile.

    B   They need little attention.

    C   They are cheap and attractive.

2   The broadcast is aimed at people

    A   who suffer from allergies.

    B   who want background plants.

    C   who neglect their gardens.

Extract Two

You hear a couple talking about their house.

3   The couple bought the farmhouse because they thought

    A   it was reasonably priced.

    B   it was in bad condition.

    C   it could be improved.

4   Using recycled wood made the kitchen look

    A   warm and sunny.

    B   more established.

    C   ultra modern.

Extract Three

You hear a woman talking about her business.

5   What does the speaker do?

  A   She supplies props for TV productions.

  B   She writes scenarios for TV serials.

  C   She sells items of stationery.

6   Her new enterprise turned out to be both

  A   engaging and meaningful.

  B   appealing and profitable.

  C   exciting and constructive.

Part 2

You will hear a report on how English has become a global language. For questions **7-15**, complete the sentences with a word or short phrase.

The spread of English around the globe means it is now termed a [_____ **7**].

English first started to spread when explorers made [_____ **8**] to the other side of the world.

The influence of Britain in the past and the influence of American businesses are the [_____ **9**] which give English its present significance.

The number of people whose [_____ **10**] is English is significantly greater in the USA than in the UK.

It is difficult to [_____ **11**] the communicative functions of English in some countries.

It is sometimes suggested that English is [_____ **12**] superior to other languages.

People tend to judge languages using subjective rather than [_____ **13**].

English sentence structure is [_____ **14**].

Language success is [_____ **15**] on a variety of different things.

Part 3

You will hear an interview with Maria Stefanovich, co-founder of a creativity group which organises workshops for executives. For questions **16-20**, choose the answer (**A, B, C** or **D**) which fits best according to what you hear.

16   Corporations appreciate mask-making workshops because

    A   no one wants negative faces at the office.

    B   unhappy employees won't come to work.

    C   they realise how their employees see them.

    D   their employees change their approach.

17   Companies are turning to creative workshops because they have acknowledged that

    A   unproductive employees are a financial burden.

    B   the traditional work environment has its limitations.

    C   there is an increase in absenteeism.

    D   employees are working too hard without enjoying it.

18   The employees at the firm 'Play'

    A   change positions frequently to lessen boredom.

    B   have business cards indicating their jobs.

    C   dress up like comic book characters.

    D   do not have stereotyped ideas about their jobs.

19   The companies that show most interest in creative workshops are surprising because

    A   they usually have creative employees to begin with.

    B   their employees are the ones who have to present regularly.

    C   there are many other exciting workshops they would prefer.

    D   their employees should be used to being funny.

20   Maria mentions the traditional companies that have held workshops in order to

    A   boast about the clients her company has helped.

    B   show that they have a narrow list of clients.

    C   downplay the serious reputations of the firms.

    D   point out the diversity of those trying different approaches.

Part 4

You will hear five short extracts in which different people are talking about how they travel.

Task One

For questions **21-25**, choose from the list (**A-H**) how each speaker prefers to travel.

Task Two

For questions **26-30**, choose from the list (**A-H**) what each speaker says about the advantages of the way they travel.

You will hear the recording twice. While you listen, you must complete both tasks.

A	in an unhurried way when it's for leisure			**A**	not having to queue up at airports		
B	only for business, never for pleasure	Speaker 1	21	**B**	the short and relaxing journeys	Speaker 1	26
C	with the bare minimum of belongings	Speaker 2	22	**C**	getting a deep insight into places visit	Speaker 2	27
		Speaker 3	23			Speaker 3	28
D	using their own personal transport	Speaker 4	24	**D**	learning new languages	Speaker 4	29
E	by taking extended independent holidays	Speaker 5	25	**E**	getting a real feeling of liberty	Speaker 5	30
F	by avoiding long distance travel			**F**	avoiding delays on arrival		
G	on package holidays			**G**	experiencing the slow pace of the journey		
H	without taking any luggage			**H**	enjoying the thrill of danger		

24

Paper 4 – Speaking *(approx. 16 minutes)*

The speaking test involves two candidates and two examiners. One examiner, the Interlocutor, will speak to you while the other, the Assessor, will just listen.

Part 1 *(2 minutes)*

You will be asked questions in turn about certain aspects of your personal life; where you are from, what you do for a living, where you go to school, your hobbies and your general opinion on certain topics.

Part 2 *(4 minutes)*

You will be asked to discuss the photographs on page **129** together. There are two stages in this part.

Stage 1
Here are some photographs depicting people with different lifestyles. Look at pictures 2 and 4 on page 129 and talk together about the different ways of life the people shown here might have.

Stage 2
Now look at all the pictures. Imagine these photographs will be part of an advertising campaign for a new product. Talk together about the kind of product each of these photographs could be used to promote and select the best photograph for an advertising campaign.

Part 3 *(10 minutes)*

You will be asked to talk on your own, comment on what your partner says and join in a three-way discussion with your partner and the Interlocutor around a certain theme.

Tourism

Candidate A will be asked to look at **prompt card (a)** and talk about it for two minutes.
There are also some ideas on the card to use, if the candidate wishes.

Prompt Card (a)
Why is tourism important today?
– international understanding
– national economies
– improvement of facilities

Candidate B will then be asked a question related to the topic:
• *How does tourism benefit local people and economies?*
Then the Interlocutor will invite Candidate A to join in using the following prompt:
• *What do you think?*

Candidate B will then be given **prompt card (b)** and asked to discuss it for two minutes.
There are also some ideas on the card to use, if the candidate wishes.

Prompt Card (b)
Why do tourists come to your country?
– natural beauty
– entertainment
– history

Candidate A will then be asked a question related to the topic:
• *Is tourism affordable in your country?*
Then the Interlocutor will invite Candidate B to join in using the following prompt:
• *Do you agree?*

The test will then be concluded with a number of general questions about the topic:
• *What negative effects might an increase in tourism produce?*
• *How has tourism affected the diet of local people?*
• *How successful would eco-tourism be in your country?*
• *What features could make an area attractive to visitors?*

Paper 1 – Reading & Use of English *(1 hour 30 minutes)*

Part 1

For questions **1-8**, read the text below and decide which answer (**A, B, C** or **D**) best fits each gap. Mark your answers **on the separate answer sheet**.

There is an example at the beginning (**0**).

0   **A**   pile   **B**   bunch   **C**   crowd   **D**   heap

0	A	B	C	D

Making The Magnificent Seven

Akira Kurosawa's 1954 classic *Seven Samurai* is about a (**0**) ....B..... of down-on-their-luck warriors who agree to defend a small village from a band of thieves in (**1**) .... for three meals a day and much honour. Since Kurosawa's (**2**) .... influence was the epic Westerns of John Ford, it is (**3**) .... that in 1959 Hollywood thought Samurai would make a good cowboy film – and The Magnificent Seven appeared on the screen. Originally, Yul Brynner was to direct the remake but after much (**4**) ...., director John Sturges took the (**5**) .... Aside from Broadway actor Eli Wallach, Brynner was the only famous name in the movie; Steve McQueen, Charles Bronson, Robert Vaughn and James Coburn got their career changing roles by (**6**) .... of mouth. Now, in this digitally rejigged (**7**) .... you can find out what happened on the action-filled set via an exclusive new documentary and how the film nearly did not become the (**8**) .... classic it is today.

1	**A**	reciprocity	**B**	trade	**C**	exchange	**D**	substitute
2	**A**	deep	**B**	major	**C**	large	**D**	most
3	**A**	sarcastic	**B**	ironic	**C**	mocking	**D**	derisive
4	**A**	argument	**B**	combat	**C**	brawling	**D**	jostling
5	**A**	steering	**B**	pilot	**C**	handle	**D**	helm
6	**A**	talk	**B**	speech	**C**	word	**D**	claim
7	**A**	model	**B**	recital	**C**	variety	**D**	version
8	**A**	idolised	**B**	revered	**C**	sacred	**D**	worshipped

Part 2

For questions **9-16**, read the text below and think of the word which best fits each space. Use only **one** word in each space. There is an example at the beginning (**0**). Write your answers **IN CAPITAL LETTERS on the separate answer sheet.**

Example: | 0 | B | E | E | N | | | | | | | | | | | | |

IQ Tests

Psychologists have long been interested in how we judge intelligence in strangers. Now tests have (0) ....BEEN.... designed to try to discover which cues help people to judge IQ accurately, and which cause (9) .... to get it wrong. High school pupils (10) .... filmed answering thought-provoking questions and the videos were (11) .... shown to judges who were asked to rate the students intelligence. At the same time, each student was also required to sit a standard IQ test.

Certain cues matched the (12) .... of the IQ tests more closely than others. (13) .... speaking quickly or using a lot of words caused the judges to rate the students' intelligence highly, and was reflected in the IQ tests, (14) .... cues seemed to give the judges an entirely false impression of intelligence as measured by the IQ test.

Amongst the cues that led judges to assess students as dull were factors (15) .... as halting speech or slang. Cues that led judges to view students as bright included talking loudly and using proper English. (16) ...., none of these traits correlated with measured IQ.

Part 3

For questions **17-24**, read the text below. Use the word given in capitals at the end of some of the lines to form a word that fits in the space in the same line. There is an example at the beginning **(0)**. Write your answers **IN CAPITAL LETTERS on the separate answer sheet**.

Example: | **0** | V | A | R | I | A | T | I | O | N | S | | | | | | | | | |

El Nino

El Nino and La Nina are climate patterns that occur across the tropical Pacific

Ocean approximately every five years. The two **(0)** V̲A̲R̲I̲A̲T̲I̲O̲N̲S̲ work in tandem   **VARY**

and are responsible for ocean warming and cooling **(17)** ....

But it is the warming effect of El Nino that has the greatest impact around the   **RESPECT**

world.

El Nino is **(18)** .... by prolonged differences in ocean   **CHARACTER**

temperatures   in   comparison   to   the   average   value.   This

(19) .... occurs at intervals of three to seven years. The   **NORMAL**

(20) .... climate changes can have a devastating effect on   **RESULT**

developing countries dependent on **(21)** .... produce or   **AGRICULTURE**

fishing for their economies. It is probably the cause of higher degrees of rainfall

in parts of Africa, Australia and Northern Europe, while causing

(22) .... colder winters in parts of North America. Because of   **CONSIDER**

the   increased   rainfall,   El Nino   is   linked   to   increases   in   the

(23) .... of   diseases   caused   by   mosquitos.   **TRANSMIT**

(24) .... have also found a link between El Nino and an   **RESEARCH**

increased risk of conflict.

Part 4

For questions **25-30**, complete the second sentence so that it has a similar meaning to the first sentence, using the word given. **Do not change the word given.** You must use between **three** and **eight** words, including the word given. Here is an example **(0)**.

Example:

0 We are able to afford a holiday, because I was promoted.

result

As ...., we are able to afford a holiday.

0	*a result of my promotion*

Write **only** the missing words **on the separate answer sheet.**

---

25 Dawn's boss is constantly criticising her work.

fault

Dawn's boss .... her work.

26 Peter is really looking forward to starting his sky-diving course.

hardly

Peter .... his sky-diving course.

27 For the contract to be a valid legal document, both parties must sign it.

binding

For the contract .... both parties.

28 My neighbour assumes that he can use my lawnmower whenever he likes.

granted

My neighbour .... him to use my lawnmower whenever he likes.

29 If he hadn't encouraged me, I would never have entered the competition.

thanks

It was .... entered the competition.

30 Accepting retirement is often difficult.

terms

It is often .... retirement.

Part 5

You are going to read an extract from an article about Marco Polo's 'The Description of the World'. For questions **31-36**, choose the answer (**A**, **B**, **C** or **D**) which you think fits best according to the text. Mark your answers **on the separate answer sheet**.

Marco Polo

"Here begins the introduction of this book, which is called 'The Description of the World.' Lords, Emperors, and Kings, Dukes, and Marquesses, Counts, Knights, and Burgesses, and all people who wish to know the different generations of men and the diversities of the different regions of the world, then take this book and have it read and here you will find all the greatest marvels and the great diversities ..."

So begins Marco Polo's book, 'The Description of the World,' as presented in Arthur Christopher Moule's masterful English translation of a version of Marco Polo's book known to scholars as the 'F' text. The storied Venetian trader escaped bandits, pirates, rampaging rivers and sandstorms on his epic eastbound journey. Sailing the treacherous coasts of Southeast Asia and India, Marco Polo returned to Venice in 1295, after 24 years, rich in gems, and wild tales of unimagined lands. Shortly after his return to Venice, Marco Polo was captured at sea, possibly by pirates. One tradition suggests he was imprisoned in Genoa's Palazzo and that he devoted his prison time to composing his book. On his deathbed in 1324, the legendary adventurer reflected that he had many more stories to tell.

'The Description of the World,' the original product of Marco Polo's collaboration with a romance writer named Rustichello has been lost, and so scholars are left to sift through the some 150 versions known to exist, no two exactly alike. Scholars divide the 150 versions into two groups, labeled 'A' and 'B'. The 'F' text, which falls into the 'A' group, is housed in the Bibliothèque Nationale in Paris. Considered one of the best and very close to the original, it is written in a Franco-Italian language described by one scholar as 'uncouth French much mingled with Italian.'

Some of these 'A' texts are notorious for variations that show the biases, mistakes and editorial judgments of their copiers. For example, when some translators were presented with the news that the three Magi were buried at Saveh in Persia rather than in Cologne, they inserted that the people of Saveh tell many lies. As these books were translated from language to language, the opportunities for error multiplied; one text from the early

16th century is a Tuscan translation of a Latin translation of an earlier Tuscan translation of the original Franco-Italian language. Although we have no confirmation of the Marco-Rustichello collaboration other than the book itself, Marco Polo seems to have approved of at least some of its versions, for in 1307 he presented a French translation of it to an envoy of Charles of Valois.

The second group of manuscripts, known as the 'B' group, provides some provocative material not found in the 'A' texts. From this 'B' group, for example, we learn that the people around Yarkand in western China suffer from goitre — a problem for them even today. Until the 1930s the only examples of 'B' texts were a few odd bits of manuscript and a printed text by Giambattista Ramusio that appeared in 1559, two years after his death. Ramusio tells his readers that his Italian version was produced 'with the help of different copies.' The foundation of his work appears to be a Latin text dating from before 1320, with influences from other identifiable versions. What is distinctive about Ramusio's work is that about twenty per cent of it was, until 1932, considered unique. That twenty per cent is thought to have come from another early Latin text, which may have been destroyed in a 1557 fire. In any event, the source has never been found.

A second version containing much of Ramusio's original material surfaced in Toledo, Spain in 1932. Most of this Latin manuscript agrees with the 'F' manuscript, but it also contains some 200 passages not found in 'F'. About 120 of those, however, are found in Ramusio's book. Because the remaining 80 offer valuable historical and geographical material and even help to clarify some obscure passages of 'F', this manuscript is thought to be a copy of something that was very close to an original.

In sorting this out, scholars have come to conclude that Marco Polo probably wrote two versions of his book. The second version, represented by the 'B' texts, may have been a revision and expansion done for a select group of readers who had already made their way through the first book. It is unlikely that we will ever know exactly what form the first book took, but the versions we have still make for a very good read.

31 According to the second paragraph, stories about Marco Polo's life

    A   are well-supported.

    B   are all imaginary.

    C   take place at sea.

    D   are sometimes unreliable.

32 What is the 'F' text?

    A   The authentic text written by Marco Polo and Rustichello.

    B   The script with the greatest affinity to the original source.

    C   Not one of the 150 versions of Marco's original book.

    D   A good version of the 'B' texts written in Franco-Italian.

33 What is one of the main problems with the 'A' texts?

    A   All translators manipulated the truth.

    B   Editing is now difficult and unreliable.

    C   The early versions were remote from the original text.

    D   Later translations distorted the original.

34 The 'B' group of manuscripts

    A   contained previously undocumented information.

    B   were compilations of manuscripts printed by Ramusio.

    C   dealt with health and culture in China.

    D   were published two years after Ramusio's death.

35 What was found in Spain in 1932?

    A   A Latin version containing valuable information about Ramusio.

    B   A text which largely corresponds to the 'F' manuscript.

    C   A manuscript of 200 passages that do not appear in the 'F' text.

    D   The original book written by Marco Polo.

36 In relation to the book, *'The Description of the World,'* the author suggests that

    A   despite its uncertain origins, it is a fascinating piece of literature.

    B   scholars should discover who the true author was.

    C   Marco Polo wrote many versions of the same book.

    D   Marco Polo intended his original book for an elite readership.

Part 6

You are going to read an extract from a book. Seven paragraphs have been removed from the extract. Choose from the paragraphs **A-H** the one which fits each gap (**37-43**). There is one extra paragraph which you do not need to use. **Mark your answers on the separate answer sheet.**

RAJASTHAN

One evening, by the light of an electric bulb we sat out with the villagers in the main street of a 'model village' of the command area. The street was unpaved, and the villagers, welcoming us, had quickly spread cotton rugs on the ground that had been softened by the morning's rain, half hardened by the afternoon's heat, and then trampled and manured by the village cattle returning at dusk. The women had withdrawn, we were left with the men and, until the rain came roaring in again, I talked to the men.

| 37 |

The problems of the irrigation project he was directing were not only those of salinity or the ravines or land levelling. The problem as he saw it, was the remaking of men. And this was not simply making men want something; it meant in the first place, bringing them back from the self-wounding and the special waste that come with an established destitution.

| 38 |

But if in this model village – near Kotah Town, which was fast industrialising – there had been some movement forward, Bundi, the next day, seemed to take us backward. Bundi and Kotah; to me, until this trip, they had only been beautiful names, the names of related but distinct schools of Rajasthan painting. The artistic glory of Bundi had come first in the late seventeenth century.

| 39 |

The fortifications were now useless, the palace was empty. One dark, dusty room had old photographs and remnants of Victorian bric-a-brac. The small formal garden in the courtyard was in decay; and the mechanical, decorative nineteenth-century Bundi murals around the courtyard had faded to blues and yellows and greens. In the inner rooms, hidden from the sun, brighter colours survived, and some panels were exquisite. But it all awaited ruin.

| 40 |

Their mock aggressiveness and mock exasperation held little of real despair or rebellion. It was a ritual show of deference to authority, a demonstration of their complete dependence on authority. The commissioner smiled and listened and heard them all; and their passion faded.

| 41 |

These officials were far removed from the commissioner's anxieties, from his vision of what could be done with their land. They were, really, at peace with the world they knew. Like the woman in whose yard we sat. She was friendly, she had dragged out string beds for us from her little brick hut; but her manner was slightly supercilious. There was a reason. She was happy, she considered herself blessed. She had had three sons, and she glowed with that achievement.

| 42 |

In the fall of such obvious poverty, men had retreated to their last, impregnable defences: their knowledge of who they were, their unshakeable place in the scheme of things; and this knowledge was like their knowledge of the seasons. Rituals marked the passage of each day, rituals marked every stage of a man's life. Life itself had been turned to ritual; and everything beyond this complete and sanctified world was vain and phantasmal.

| 43 |

But to those who embraced its philosophy of distress, India also offered an enduring security, its equilibrium. Only India with its great past, its civilisation, its philosophy, and its almost holy poverty, offered this truth; India was the truth. And India, for all its surface terrors, could be proclaimed, without disingenuousness or cruelty, as perfect. Not only by pauper but by prince.

A We were, as the commissioner said, among men who, until recently, cut only the very tops of sugar cane and left the rest of the plant, the substance of the crop, to rot. So the present concern, here in the model village, about fertilisers and yields was an immeasurable advance.

B Kingdoms, empires, projects like the commissioner's; they had come and gone. The monuments of ambition and restlessness littered the land, so many of them abandoned or destroyed, so many unfinished, the work of dynasties suddenly supplanted. India taught the vanity of all action; and the visitor could be appalled by the waste, and by all that now appeared to threaten the commissioner's enterprise.

C So handsome, these men of Rajasthan, so self-possessed; it took time to understand that their concerns were limited. The fields, water, crops, cattle: that was where concern began and ended. They were a model village, and so they considered themselves. There was little more that they needed, and I began to see my own ideas of village improvement as fantasies. Nothing beyond food – and survival – had, as yet, become an object of ambition. As the commissioner well knew.

D All vitality had been sucked up into that palace on the hill; and now vitality had gone out of Bundi. It showed in the rundown town on the hillside below the palace; it showed in the fields; it showed in the people, more beaten down than at Kotah Town just sixty miles away, less amenable to the commissioner's ideas, and more full of complaints. They complained even when they had no cause; and it seemed that they complained because they felt it was expected of them.

E All the chivalry of Rajasthan had been reduced here to nothing. The palace was empty; the petty wars of princes had been absorbed into legend and could no longer be dated. All that remained was what the visitor could see: small poor fields, ragged men, huts, monsoon mud. But in that very abjectness lay security. Where the world had shrunk, and ideas of human possibility had become extinct, the world could be seen as complete.

F But as self satisfied as she was the Prince's state, or what had been his state, was wretched; just the palace and the peasants. The developments in which he had invested hadn't yet begun to show. In the morning, in the rain, I saw young child labourers using their hands alone to shovel gravel onto a waterlogged path. Groundnuts were the only source of protein here; but the peasants preferred to sell their crop, and the children were stunted.

G And after the flat waterlogged fields, pallid paddy thinning out at times to marshland, after the desolation of the road from Kotah, the flooded ditches, the occasional cycle-rickshaw, the damp groups of bright-turbaned peasants waiting for the bus, Bundi Castle on its hill was startling, its great walls like the work of giants, the extravagant creation of men who had once had much to defend.

H Later we sat with the 'village level' officially in the shade of a small tree in a woman's yard. They were the last in the chain of command; on them much of the success of the scheme depended. There had been evidence during the morning's tour that they hadn't all been doing their jobs. But they were not abashed; instead, sitting in a line on a string bed, dressed like officials in trousers and shirts, they spoke of their need for promotion and status.

Part 7

You are going to read four extracts which are all concerned in some way with marriage and weddings. For questions **44-53**, choose from the sections (**A-D**). The sections may be chosen more than once.

Mark your answers **on the separate answer sheet**.

In which section are the following mentioned?

possible friction between relatives	44 ....
a traditional skill that has been lost to a certain extent	45 ....
the quick reversal of a decision	46 ....
the consideration of ways to encourage families to stay intact	47 ....
a comparison to imagery from old films	48 ....
a traditional oath that is now rarely used	49 ....
the function of religion in helping society be better	50 ....
punishing people for failing relationships	51 ....
a sudden realisation of the unsuitability of a partner	52 ....
the significance of a tradition associated with marriage	53 ....

A Wedding Arrangements

Royal Lily Weddings exists to provide you with a professional wedding co-ordination service.

1 We can attend to all aspects of the event. Rest assured no detail will be disregarded by us.

2 Not everyone gets married in church these days. Even the traditional sometimes choose other venues they consider more romantic or fitting – a beautiful garden for instance, or a beach, or a mountain top - even a bus shelter.

3 Choice regarding the dress too, has become far wider. If you don't want to be married in white, dare to be bold. We offer advice and access to select couturiers and fashion designers.

4 When it comes to the ceremony itself, and depending on who officiates, you can more or less write the book. The traditional Christian vow made by a wife to her husband has largely been abandoned, and in its wake, personalised vows have come to the fore.

5 Seating at the reception, as at the church, can be a problem. We will liaise between you and any unintentionally difficult family members or friends using tact and discretion to preserve the harmony on the day as well as in the years to follow.

Whatever format you choose, do come to Royal Lily Weddings to make sure it all adds up to a day you will remember for the rest of your lives.

B The State of Family Life

An important role of the church is to remind us of the moral concerns confronting society. Recently we have been reminded of that role in a speech given by the archbishop, who lamented the high rate of divorce and linked falling fertility rates to the collapse of traditional family life. He predicted that the lower birth rate would have serious social consequences in the future and suggested that the tax system be used to reward couples who stay together and have children.

It is unlikely, however, that imposing a 'divorce tax' on separating couples, or reintroducing fault as an element in determining custody and property settlements, as he suggested, will do much to keep families together. Using the tax system or custody laws to discipline couples whose marriages fail, will only add to the stress and hardship of those contemplating divorce. Marriage is not 'the only contract that people can walk away from without a penalty' as he suggested,

because divorce itself can be a great penalty for those affected by it. Keeping couples together by duress is not the best way to strengthen marriage. How to nurture the individual desire for growth and fulfilment, while strengthening family life, is a great challenge for all of society. The archbishop is to be congratulated for re-opening the debate.

C Mehndi

Mehndi is deeply ingrained in the Indian tradition. Although applied on other occasions as well, it is an integral part of the wedding ceremony and is almost synonymous with marriage. A special time is set aside for the application of mehndi to the hands and feet of the bride-to-be, and the ceremony generally takes place on the night before the actual wedding. In the past, when almost all the women in any given household were proficient in this art, the most talented relative or friend was usually designated to perform this duty. Now that this art is getting lost in the race for urbanisation, special beauticians or artists have to be hired for the purpose and mehndi parlours are springing up in large cities.

D Outside the Registry Office

And then she saw the Registry Office and a small crowd chatting on the pavement in front of the entrance. Like a visitor from another planet, she saw her publisher and her agent and her poor father's crazy vegetarian cousin and several of her friends and quite a few neighbours. And she saw Penelope, animated, her red hat attracting the attention of one or two of the photographers, conversing with the best man and Geoffrey. And then she saw, in a flash, but for all time, the totality of his mouse-like seemliness.

Leaning forward, in a condition of extreme calm, she said to the driver, "Would you take me on a little further please? I've changed my mind."

"Certainly, Madam he replied, thinking she was one of the guests. "Where would you like to go?"

"Perhaps round the park?" she suggested.

As the car proceeded smoothly past the Registry Office, Edith saw, as if in a still photograph, Penelope and Geoffrey, staring, their mouths open in horror. Then the scene became slightly more animated, as the crowd began to straggle down the steps, reminding her of a sequence in some early masterpiece of the cinema, now preserved as archive material.

Paper 2 – Writing *(1 hour 30 mins)*

Part 1

Read the two texts below.

Write an essay summarising and evaluating the key points from both texts. Use your own words throughout as far as possible, and include your own ideas in your answers.

Write your answer in **240-280 words on the separate answer sheet**.

1   **A Pain in the Neck**

In the middle of the twentieth century, typists started to complain of pain in their necks, shoulders and arms, and since then Repetitive Strain Injury has become a widespread problem which costs the world economy billions of pounds a year. With workers sitting at desks for eight hours a day for years on end, often with poor posture and poorly designed workspaces, it is hardly surprising that so many people develop problems. More and more companies are now calling in ergonomic consultants. They find that by following their advice productivity increases and claims for injury or illness greatly diminish.

Healthy Staff, Healthy Office

Certain characteristics of the workplace have been associated with injury. These characteristics are either environmental, e.g. temperature, lighting and noise, or task physical, which relates to the interaction between worker and environment, e.g. posture, repetition, duration and recovery time. Ergonomic solutions to these problems may include providing chairs with wrist and foot rests, moving desks to minimise glare without shutting out daylight and providing window coatings and blinds to further reduce glare in some areas. Such measures are good for employer and employee, reducing the number of injuries and working time lost, as well as cutting compensation costs.

Write your **essay**.

Part 2

Write an answer to **one** of the questions **2-4** in this part. Write your answer in **280-320** words in an appropriate style **on the separate answer sheet**. Put the question number in the box at the top of the answer sheet.

2   You are employed by a local magazine and have been asked to write a review of a new hotel which has recently opened in the town. Describe the facilities available. Give your impression of the interior decorations, service, and value for money and say whether you would recommend it or not.

Write your **review**.

3   You are a member of a group that is involved in a campaign to encourage people to help the environment. You have been asked to contribute an article for a local magazine describing how you became interested in protecting the environment and explaining how groups such as yours can help.

Write your **article**.

4   The company you work for has just completed renovation of its premises in order to make them better to work in and more attractive to clients. Write a report on what changes have been made to the premises and whether they are an improvement.

Write your **report**.

Part 1

You will hear three different extracts. For questions **1-6**, choose the answer (**A**, **B** or **C**) which fits best according to what you hear. There are two questions for each extract.

Extract One

You hear a man talking about his childhood on a council estate.

1 How does he feel about the estate where he lived?

    A He thinks too much importance was attached to housing needs.

    B He feels fortunate to have grown up there.

    C He resents the lack of play facilities for children.

2 How did he and his friends feel about having to make their own entertainment?

    A They didn't like being left to their own devices.

    B They just went ahead and enjoyed themselves.

    C They were too busy working to think about it.

Extract Two

You hear a man talking about bird-watching and the best ways to attract wild birds.

3 The speaker says that many different birds can be persuaded to come if you

    A put out water for wild birds.

    B visit an area regularly.

    C provide a variety of foodstuffs.

4 The speaker says that in order to choose an observation point you should

    A visit it as often and as regularly as possible.

    B find somewhere in your neighbourhood.

    C look for an area that has everything birds need.

Extract Three

You hear part of a sports programme on the radio.

5 What was the 'disastrous start' referred to by the speaker?

A Accidents involving two horses.

B Riders having to abandon their horses.

C The bad condition of the course.

6 What do show organisers hold responsible for the poor conditions?

A The limited amount of water lying on the surface.

B The building materials used in making the course.

C The extremely muddy ground.

Part 2

You will hear a radio programme about a family who gave up their suburban lifestyle for a life in the country. For questions **7-15**, complete the sentences with a word or short phrase.

Moving away from the town was made possible when Evan received his [_____ 7].

Their house has [_____ 8] views of the countryside.

Their main priority is to make themselves [_____ 9] before putting their own produce on the market.

Until they can live off the profits of the land the couple are looking for [_____ 10].

For the time being Nina is starting to make a(n) [_____ 11].

Many people like them, who are [_____ 12] with their jobs, have moved to the country.

They invested in a TV set for the [_____ 13] of their daughter.

The couple find their new way of life extremely [_____ 14].

This kind of life is demanding so it is important to be [_____ 15] to make it work.

Part 3

You will hear an interview with Haile Gebrselassie who has won two Olympic gold medals. For questions **16-20**, choose the answer (**A**, **B**, **C** or **D**) which fits best according to what you hear.

16 Runners from Ethiopia and other Rift Valley countries have an advantage because

    A Ethiopians like running for its own sake.

    B they train from an early age.

    C their bodies have adapted to their environment.

    D they run up the mountains.

17 Runners from other countries may suffer

    A during training in the mountains.

    B due to bad circulation.

    C when they leave high altitudes.

    D due to insufficient training.

18 Haile is particularly good at the distance of 10 kilometres because

    A he was obliged to run to school and back.

    B he was taught to run at school.

    C school in Asela had many long-distance athletes.

    D his running style was influenced by carrying books.

19 Altitude plays a part in producing top athletes, but another factor involved is

    A that children are encouraged to run by their parents.

    B that running is their only means of getting around.

    C the influence of the Ethiopian attitude to life.

    D the long distances between places.

20 Haile and his equipment sponsor established the Global Adidas running club because

    A they wanted to recruit more athletes in Ethiopia.

    B they wanted to invest money in the sport in Ethiopia.

    C they wanted to see more runners in the hills.

    D they wanted to bring athletes from Asela to Addis Ababa.

Part 4

You will hear five short extracts in which different people talk about their career as a performer.

Task One
For questions **21-25** choose from the list (**A-H**) how each speaker got started as a performer.

Task Two
For questions **26-30** choose from the list (**A-H**) what each speaker says they like about their profession.

You will hear the recording twice. While you listen, you must complete both tasks.

A	by beginning as an amateur	
B	by going abroad to train	Speaker 1 **21**
C	through acquiring skills whilst working	Speaker 2 **22**
D	By attending a government work programme.	Speaker 3 **23**
		Speaker 4 **24**
E	with financial support from their job	Speaker 5 **25**
F	through gaining recognition as a star	
G	by changing their style of performance	
H	through the encouragement of one family member	

A	earning enough to be comfortable	
B	working long productive hours	Speaker 1 **26**
C	altering people's perception of their work	Speaker 2 **27**
		Speaker 3 **28**
D	the greater flexibility of expression in their art	Speaker 4 **29**
E	having leisure time and high earnings	Speaker 5 **30**
F	not having to go abroad to work	
G	receiving satisfaction from creativity	
H	being away from home as much as possible	

Paper 4 – Speaking *(approx. 16 minutes)*

The speaking test involves two candidates and two examiners. One examiner, the Interlocutor, will speak to you while the other, the Assessor, will just listen.

Part 1 *(2 minutes)*

You will be asked questions in turn about where you live and where you are from, your work, studies and interests, and your views on certain things.

Part 2 *(4 minutes)*

You will be asked to discuss the photographs on page **130** together. There are two stages in this part.

Stage 1
Here are some photographs which show animals in the wild and in some form of captivity. Look at pictures 1 and 2 on page 130 and discuss the differences in the ways the animals live.

Stage 2
You belong to a group which wishes to promote better treatment of animals. Discuss how each of these images might help in your campaign. Then select two pictures which would be most effective on a poster.

Part 3 *(10 minutes)*

You will be asked to talk on your own, comment on what your partner says and join in a three-way discussion with your partner and the Interlocutor around a certain theme.

People

Candidate A will be asked to look at **prompt card (a)** and talk about it for two minutes.
There are also some ideas on the card to use, if the candidate wishes.

Prompt Card (a)
How important is social status to people today?
– increased demands
– the mass media
– money

Candidate B will then be asked a question related to the topic:
• *Do you think people are pushed to achieve nowadays?*
Then the Interlocutor will invite Candidate A to join in using the following prompt:
• *How about you?*

Candidate B will then be given **prompt card (b)** and asked to discuss it for two minutes.
There are also some ideas on the card to use, if the candidate wishes.

Prompt Card (b)
To what extent were your grandparents happier in their everyday lives than your parents?
– the rat race
– health and education
– materialism and greed

Candidate A will then be asked a question related to the topic:
• *Are people happier nowadays?*
Then the Interlocutor will invite Candidate B to join in using the following prompt:
• *Do you agree?*

The test will then be concluded with a number of general questions about the topic:
• *What are the advantages of rejecting the modern lifestyle and returning to the past?*
• *Have people sacrificed personal happiness in their fight to 'keep up with the Joneses'?*
• *To what extent do you think people get what they want in life?*
• *What are the advantages and disadvantages of living in an extended family environment?*

Paper 1 – Reading & Use of English (*1 hour 30 minutes*)

Part 1

For questions **1-8**, read the text below and decide which answer (**A**, **B**, **C** or **D**) best fits each gap.
Mark your answers **on the separate answer sheet**.

There is an example at the beginning (**0**).

0   **A**   abdicated   **B**   abandoned   **C**   absconded   **D**   discarded

0	A	B	C	D
	☐	▣	☐	☐

The Rothschilds

When, in the 18th century, Mayer Amschel Rothschild **(0)** .....*B*.... his studies to join a banking firm in his **(1)** .... Frankfurt, he took the first steps towards creating one of the most successful, and most influential, banks.

For nearly two centuries, the fortunes of the British government and those of the bank were fundamentally **(2)** .... Thanks to the Rothschilds, the Duke of Wellington was able to pay his army in 1814-15 (the bank received a 2% commission on the deal). Ten years later, the Rothschilds again came to the **(3)** .... when 145 British banks failed, helping prevent the **(4)** .... of the whole UK banking system.

The 19th century Prime Minister, Benjamin Disraeli, **(5)** .... one of his great political **(6)** .... to be the acquisition of enough shares in the Suez Canal to secure Britain a controlling **(7)** .... Again, thanks to a £4 million Rothschild loan. Today, the company **(8)** .... among the world's largest privately owned banks, with 40 offices in 30 different countries.

1	A	domestic	B	congenital	C	native	D	indigenous
2	A	bound	B	fastened	C	bonded	D	linked
3	A	deliverance	B	rescue	C	salvation	D	relief
4	A	subsidence	B	descent	C	collapse	D	demolition
5	A	observed	B	beheld	C	believed	D	watched
6	A	coups	B	battles	C	actions	D	exploits
7	A	benefit	B	interest	C	profit	D	activity
8	A	ranks	B	classes	C	ranges	D	positions

Part 2

For questions **9-16**, read the text below and think of the word which best fits each space. Use only **one** word in each space. There is an example at the beginning (**0**). Write your answers **IN CAPITAL LETTERS on the separate answer sheet**.

Example: | **0** | O | F | | | | | | | | | | | | | | |

BAZAARS

Originally a public market district (**0**) ....OF....... a Persian town, bazaars soon spread to Arabia, Turkey and North Africa. In current English usage, it refers to (**9**) .... a single shop or concession selling miscellaneous items and to a fair at (**10**) .... such miscellany is sold.

The family bazaar of the ancient Islamic nations is vividly described in 'The Thousand and One Nights' folktales. It is a distinct quarter of the town (**11**) .... which access is forbidden after sundown. Such a bazaar may be divided into districts, (**12**) .... all purveyors of one type of merchandise grouped together.

While the bazaar in smaller towns (**13**) .... comprised of a single narrow street of stalls, in larger cities, like Istanbul, it is by (**14**) .... means simple, consisting of many miles of passageways. Some bazaars, such as the ones built at Sashan and Isfahan in the 17th century, were designed with great architectural integrity. They were usually roofed for protection from the sun, (**15**) .... by a single roof of vaulted domes or with awnings. Most of these ancient bazaars have been gradually modernised (**16**) .... the centuries.

Part 3

For questions **17-24**, read the text below. Use the word given in capitals at the end of some of the lines to form a word that fits in the space in the same line. There is an example at the beginning (**0**). Write your answers **IN CAPITAL LETTERS on the separate answer sheet.**

Example: | **0** | C | O | M | P | A | N | I | O | N | S | H | I | P | | | | | |

The Cat

The house cat, Felis catus, is a small furry animal much valued by humans for

both **(0)** .C.O.M.P.A.N.I.O.N.S.H.I.P. and its skill at hunting vermin. Although there is   **COMPANY**

some **(17)** .... as to when cats and humans first   **CERTAIN**

developed a symbiotic relationship, there have been instances of cat

(18) .... since as early as the Neolithic era, at least. It is   **DOMESTIC**

believed that cats may have an inborn **(19)** .... towards   **DISPOSE**

tameness and, according to some **(20)** .... may have   **RESEARCH**

actively sought human company and inveigled their way into early human

(21) .... It is debatable as to whether cats were really   **SETTLE**

valued for their ability to keep pest numbers down but there is no doubt that

there are few creatures who can hunt as **(22)** ....   **GRACE**

With lithe, flexible bodies and sharp **(23)** .... claws, cats   **RETRACT**

are eminently suited to stealth attacks on prey and are **(24)** ....   **EXAMPLE**

predators.

Part 4

For questions **25-30**, complete the second sentence so that it has a similar meaning to the first sentence, using the word given. **Do not change the word given.** You must use between **three** and **eight** words, including the word given. Here is an example (**0**).

Example:

0   We are able to afford a holiday, because I was promoted.

result

As ...., we are able to afford a holiday.

0	*a result of my promotion*

Write only the missing words **on the separate answer sheet.**

---

25   I expected the book to be far better because it had been written by such a good novelist.

short

The book .... it had been written by such a good novelist.

26   Such rudeness to a stranger cannot possibly be justified.

excuse

There .... rude to a stranger.

27 If anyone can get lost, he will.

depended

He .... get lost.

28 Philip rarely bothers about what other people think.

takes

Philip .... what other people think.

29 Protective clothing must be worn when entering this area.

forbidden

It .... protective clothing.

30 There will be no progress until we have fully understood the problem.

full

Not until there is .... be any progress.

Part 5

You are going to read an article about lenses used in painting. For questions **31-36**, choose the answer (**A**, **B**, **C** or **D**) which you think fits best according to the text. Mark your answers **on the separate answer sheet**.

Photography and Old Masters

David Hockney's breakthrough work on the use made by the old masters of mirrors and lenses is becoming well known. Though there are carpers and hecklers, it has leapt from hunch, through theory, more or less to accepted fact, in a remarkably short time. His basic idea, that the use of lenses – effectively photography without the chemical fixing – spread throughout European painting from the Renaissance onwards, alters forever our own perception of some of the greatest artists in history.

Two years ago, Hockney was at the National Gallery's Ingrès show in London. He was gripped with curiosity at the speed, accuracy and odd certainties of Ingrès' extraordinarily fast portrait sketches done in Rome and thought Ingrès might have used an optical device called a camera lucida. Hockney obtained one and, with its help, was soon also doing very fast, accurate pencil portraits. The more paintings Hockney studied, the more evidence he found that lenses were used. This is not to say that the great names in Western art were cheating. Why is using a lens cheating, any more than using a plumb line? But they were certainly being helped ... with photography.

When I met Hockney in his London studio, he was flinging out ideas. 'The photograph is far, far older than we think. It's just that they didn't have the chemical fixative until the nineteenth century,' he says. 'It frees us. It makes the artists of the past much closer. They were marvellous artists and their techniques have a great deal to teach the artists of today.'

Hockney created a massive gallery of photos and postcards of paintings on a wall of his Californian studio, running from the 1300s to the last century, divided into Northern and Southern European, along which breakthroughs in realism become strikingly obvious. Each, he thinks, corresponds to a new technological breakthrough in lens making, with the first around 1420. That is well known and much discussed. But why did it happen? Hockney chuckles in derision; 'Oh, they say, suddenly in 1420 everyone could draw better. From that moment you never see a badly drawn basket again in Western art. They are suddenly all perfectly woven, in perfect perspective. The answer is in fact the new lenses that spread from the Low Countries to Florence and then the rest of Italy.'

Lenses show movement; the projections, hundreds of years ago, are far better than high-definition television. In clarity and colour, they are amazing, but they could not be preserved, except by drawing. They were living projections. There is no doubt that painters saw colour images, optical projections which look like paintings, and they made paintings which look like optical projections. The old masters saw moving colour pictures.

Hockney pursued the theory with art historians and friends. From everywhere, the evidence accumulated. A mere artist, a hand, brush and pencil man, seemed to have spotted what the combined intellects of academic art history had missed. It sounds, at first hearing, a complex theory. But here is the simple version. Think of three periods of art history, all defined by photography. First, the use of lenses from the Renaissance to the mid-nineteenth century. A trick of the artist's trade, not much talked about to laymen. Second, the arrival of chemically fixed photography, which immediately threatens the painters' trade. Artists respond by either trying to turn back to the pre-lens era or by emphasising an anti-photographic style of painting. The third phase, through which we are living today, is that of the computer.

The computer allows the manipulation of the photographic image. Chemical photography gives way to digital technology, which can be infinitely manipulated and manipulation means drawing. Since photographs are going to be increasingly made by drawing, the photograph has really lost its veracity.

Here, triumphantly, the Hockney case that the great masters used lenses comes full circle, returning us in 2001 to the revival of drawing, another life-long passion. 'For 400, nearly 500 years, the hand was involved with the camera. Artists were using the lens. Then for 160 years, you had chemical photography. But that has now come to an end, and with digital photography, you have got the hand back in the camera. This is why photography is changing and actually moving back towards drawing and painting.' And Hockney leans back and laughs. As well he might.

31 The result of David Hockney's work is that

   A   the theory has been accepted too quickly.

   B   it is no longer understood how these artists painted.

   C   the work of well-known artists has been discredited.

   D   the artists' works must be viewed differently.

32 The writer takes pains not to suggest that the painters were cheating because

   A   Hockney could do fast, accurate pencil drawings using lenses.

   B   he considers the use of lenses an acceptable technique.

   C   as the paintings were studied, it became clear that lenses were used.

   D   modern day artists use photography to help them.

33 Hockney considers that drawing became better in 1420 because

   A   the improvement corresponded with the first improvement in lens-making.

   B   the depiction of objects suddenly gained greater importance in art.

   C   each breakthrough in realism corresponded with a breakthrough in lens-making.

   D   new types of lenses spread across Italy from then onwards.

34 How did artists react when fixed photography was introduced?

   A   They attempted to paint their subjects more realistically.

   B   They responded by using lenses themselves to paint.

   C   They turned to a more abstract style.

   D   They began using computers instead of a camera.

35 What does the writer mean when he says that photography has 'lost its veracity' (line 37)?

   A   Digital technology is increasingly being used in photography.

   B   Artists are using computers to produce their work instead of brushes.

   C   Photographs cannot be relied upon to give a true representation.

   D   Digital technology allows images to be changed by hand.

36 The purpose of the text is to

   A   demonstrate the limitations of Hockney's theory.

   B   explain how art was affected by developments in technology.

   C   show that Hockney is more intelligent than art historians.

   D   prove that cameras were used in renaissance art.

Part 6

You are going to read an article about the Spanish treasure fleets. Seven paragraphs have been removed from the extract. Choose from the paragraphs **A-H** the one which fits each gap (**37-43**). There is one extra paragraph which you do not need to use. **Mark your answers on the separate answer sheet.**

Spanish Treasure

Gold earrings hung with pearls sank with a Spanish galleon west of Havana, one of the many wrecked by pirates, storms and treacherous reefs. These and other artefacts offer a wealth of clues about the history of Cuba's golden past. A glittering fortune in gold and silver has been recovered from the sea floor. Treasures including luxuries such as rare wood and exotic feathers were shipped from the New World to Seville by way of Cuba.

37

In a typical year, the first of the two annual treasure fleets left Spain in spring and entered the Caribbean near the island of Margarita, off Venezuela — a source of pearls and a frequent target of pirates. Here the flotilla usually split in two, following courses that touched much of the Spanish New World. One convoy stopped at ports along the Spanish Main, as the English called the northern coast of South America and the Caribbean islands. Colonists, forbidden to manufacture anything, had to buy even such ordinary items as cutlery, tools and religious medals from the convoy.

38

In late summer, the merchant ships and war ships sailed to Havana's well-fortified harbour to form the treasure fleet. Theoretically, the captain general and his warships defended all the merchantmen against pirates. In reality, storms frequently scattered the flotilla making individual ships vulnerable. Pirates chose these loners to attack and loot. But Piet Heyn, to the Spanish a pirate, to the Dutch a fabled admiral, was not satisfied with picking off the stragglers. He wanted the whole treasure.

39

Officials in Havana, who feared this legendary figure more than any other foe, kept watch for him, especially when a treasure fleet was about to sail for Spain. On August 4, 1628, Heyn and his ships lay off Cuba, not sure whether the treasure fleet's Mexican component (the Dutch called it the silver fleet) had left for Havana to link up with the rest of the flotilla. Spanish scout vessels spotted the Dutch and sent swift courier ships to Veracruz

to warn Juan de Benavides, captain general of the treasure fleet. But, unknown to the Spanish, Heyn had captured one of the courier ships. Now aware that his prey would soon arrive off Cuba, Heyn waited to pounce.

40

Finally in August, he set sail again. As he neared Matanzas Bay, about 50 miles east of Havana, he saw more than 30 Dutch warships bearing down on him. 'I continued my course, resolved to die,' Benavides bravely wrote in a letter to the king. But another officer later testified that Benavides had foolishly led the fleet into the bay. In his panic, he grounded his own ship and all that followed.

41

'I jumped into a boat,' Benavides later recounted, claiming he had arranged in vain for his ship to be set afire in his absence. Leoz, seeing his ship boarded by the Dutchmen, ran below, changed into the clothes of an ordinary sailor, and slipped in among the crewmen who already had laid down their muskets.

42

That done, Heyn put his men aboard the six looted galleons, along with three others, and sent them off to the Netherlands in the wake of the nine he had captured earlier. Benavides' flagship, so jammed with cargo that the cannon ports were obstructed, had 29 guns; Leoz's had 22. Neither had fired a shot.

43

The story of Heyn's triumph and Benavides' death is preserved in the General Archives of the Indies in Seville, Spain. Treasure searchers begin here, sifting through the voluminous records that officials kept on every flotilla, on every ship and every cargo. Even though the locations are sometimes imprecise, the searchers press on, going from document to hunch, from the shelves in Seville to the waters off Havana.

A Their pursuers rapidly closed in, anchored or grounded their ships, boarded boats manned with musketeers and headed for the hapless Spanish ships. The Dutch swarmed aboard Benavides' ship and the ship of Admiral Don Juan de Leoz, second in command of the flotilla.

B Spain's long reign in the New World is chronicled in archives, tucked away in endless shelves in the vaulted, echoing halls of a stately 17th century building. Included in these archival treasures are intriguing charts and maps from the 16th and 17th century, vividly portraying the harbour of Havana. Here historians and treasure hunters plough through documents which bear witness to Spain's and Cuba's turbulent marine history.

C The Netherlands hailed Heyn as a hero and cast a commemorative medal from the silver. Long afterward children sang a song — 'He has won the Silver Fleet, hurrah, hurrah, hurrah!' Benavides and Leoz returned to Spain in disgrace. Leoz was imprisoned for life. Benavides was tried, not for loss of the treasure fleet but for cowardice, and later executed. Heyn did not last long as a hero. In 1629, while attacking pirates in the English Channel, he was killed by a cannonball.

D Other ships carrying similar cargoes sailed into Cartagena, Colombia, and then west to Portobelo, Panama, the collecting point for the silver that flowed in from the mines of Peru. One day, a Dominican friar in Portobelo counted 200 mules laden with silver, which was stacked in the marketplace 'like heaps of stones in the street.'

E Flushed with a previous success — they had already captured nine ships of the silver fleet — Heyn and his men seized half a dozen Spanish ships and put the Spaniards ashore. In the days that followed, the Dutch sailors inventoried and transferred the 'large amount of plunder present,' which included 46 tons of silver.

F Hundreds of ships sank in Cuban waters, victims of pirates, war, storms or bad navigation. These are the ships sought today in the hope of finding the richest prize in the Cuban seas: ships of the Spanish treasure fleets, the flotillas which carried New World gold, silver and gems to the royal court of Spain. The flotillas first sailed into history in the 16th century when Spain's powerful Casa de Contratacion (House of Trade) ordered merchant ships to travel in convoy, guarded by armed warships.

G As a young privateer in Spanish waters, he had been captured and sentenced to be a galley slave. Freed in a prisoner exchange, he returned to sea and sought vengeance. In 1623 and 1626, as a Dutch admiral fighting against Spain for his homeland, he led rampages against Spanish America, sacking the Cuban port of Matanzas and capturing many ships.

H Scion of a wealthy family of shipbuilders, Juan de Benavides was an admiral who had never fought a sea battle. He got his appointment through influence, not skill. Benavides, shepherding about 20 ships, had left Veracruz for Havana in July, but was forced back to port because of what he described as 'an emergency' that had dismasted his flagship.

Part 7

You are going to read extracts related to children and their development.
For questions **44-53**, choose from the sections **(A-E)**. The sections may be chosen more than once.

Mark your answers **on the separate answer sheet**.

In which section are the following mentioned?

the insecurity created by being inexperienced at child rearing	**44** ....
finding ways to improve therapies for adults mistreated in childhood	**45** ....
the humiliation caused by feeling disconnected from a peer group	**46** ....
someone who only considered their own feelings about an upcoming event	**47** ....
recognising levels of educational ability	**48** ....
the susceptibility of neglected children to particular disorders	**49** ....
how external conditions can relate to maturation	**50** ....
having to accept an inability to see things from others' perspective	**51** ....
the variety of ways to ensure educational development.	**52**
how rudimentary a child's perspective can be	**53** ....

Children and their Development

A Tears and Fears

Like many parents I had not fully appreciated the emotional upheaval going to school for the first time involves for a child. I had tended to focus on my own feelings, and notwithstanding my awareness that this was a major step in my daughter's life, my own reluctant acceptance of this as a rite of passage which signalled the end of babyhood had preoccupied me to the exclusion of all else. Never once did I imagine she would have any objections.

To be fair to myself, this was partly because, having gone back to work relatively soon after she was born, I had had to leave her at home in the care of a childminder from a very early age, so she was quite a sociable child. What I had failed to appreciate, though, was the strong sense of place young children possess. To my daughter, what mattered, perhaps more than anything else, was the shift to a new, possibly threatening environment. Perhaps it is impossible for adults, to understand how primitive small children still are in the their reactions to the world around them. The world is unchanging, permanent and any alteration can represent an enormous tragedy.

B Growing up

My friends were quite envious of my having famous parents. That set me apart. At other times though, I could be terribly embarrassed by the fact that my parents weren't the same as everyone else's. I think that growing up you want to fit into some pattern, but you don't see a big enough picture to know what that pattern really is. You just see a very narrow social pattern into which you have been put and if you are spilling out over that in some way, it can be very embarrassing for a child.

I would love childhood to mean a sort of free growing, but in reality it never is because all children have dark corners which they keep to themselves. There is never that openness – it's just the nature of the beasts, both parents and children. The one cannot actually see life from the perspective of the other, and so the 'dark corners' become caverns of misunderstanding at times. It's only when you're grown up that you can actually come to terms with those misunderstandings and see your parents as they really are. Similarly, parents looking at children see them as people they love, people they have to protect from the world and people for whom they have *their* particular expectations. There are of course marvellous moments of great happiness; but there are also inescapable pains and disappointments.

C Early Literacy Development

This great resource gives the latest information on emerging reading and writing skills. You will get facts and background information to help you identify the stages of literacy development as well as strategies to facilitate them for future academic success. Learn about the characteristics and factors that promote or inhibit reading acquisition and writing development. This resource covers:

- stages in early reading and writing
- characteristics of delay and 'at risk' factors
- reading and writing facilitation strategies
- literacy activities
- suggestions for working with parents and families
- lists of picture books

D Post-Traumatic Stress

Child maltreatment is a major health problem in the United States, with, according to the U.S. Department of Health and Human Services, more than half a million cases of child abuse documented in 2010. It is well established that exposure to trauma greatly increases an individual's long-term vulnerability to psychiatric problems. Besides being linked to the development of post-traumatic stress disorder, it has been found that a high level of adult patients suffering from major depression, panic disorder and personality disorder were abused, either physically or psychologically, as children. Clarifying what follows from trauma and classifying the various types of abuse may provide pertinent information which could lead to better means of treatment for those individuals who were maltreated as children.

E Child Development

It's not surprising that the majority of first time parents find parenthood something of a daunting prospect. With no experience of what awaits them when raising a child, it's natural that they will be plagued by endless questions, seeking reassurance about the developmental progress of their child. However, it's worth remembering that not all questions about development can be answered with absolute precision. When is the right time for an infant to start walking and talking? There are some parameters to what is regarded as a normal time scale but there are no absolute hard and fast rules.

Every developmental stage, whether it be emotional, physical, psychological or intellectual is affected by a myriad of different factors. These include environmental ones such as nutrition, home background and the amount of stimulation a child receives. There are also genetic factors, too, and to what extent they may be exacerbated by environmental effects is a matter of some debate.

Paper 2 – Writing *(1 hour 30 mins)*

Part 1

Read the two texts below.

Write an essay summarising and evaluating the key points from both texts. Use your own words throughout as far as possible, and include your own ideas in your answers.

Write your answer in **240-280 words on the separate answer sheet**.

1

Divided by Comedy

The Office quickly became a hit TV comedy in Britain when it appeared in 2001. Shot in documentary style, it showed the workings of a dull office in which those workers who had managed to stay sane were forced to endure the awkward and immature actions of their co-workers, particularly their socially-inept boss. The British loved the uncompromising humour but when the series was remade for American viewers, the boss became more likeable and competent, and the workplace more optimistic. This is further evidence of deep-rooted differences in the humour of the two countries. All too often comedy gets lost in translation.

Universally Funny

Germans with no sense of humour and Americans who do not understand irony are common stereotypes in Britain. However, in the final report from LaughLab, a research project which set out to find the world's funniest joke, Germany came top of the humour table, laughing at the widest range of jokes. Similarly, it is not hard to find examples of American irony; popular shows like *The Simpsons* and *Curb your Enthusiasm* are full of it. Is it now time to get rid of the stereotypes and recognise that the best comedy really is universal?

Write your **essay**.

Part 2

Write an answer to **one** of the questions **2-4** in this part. Write your answer in **280-320** words in an appropriate style **on the separate answer sheet**. Put the question number in the box at the top of the answer sheet.

2 You are employed as the activities co-ordinator at the local leisure centre. Your manager has asked you to write a report on the success of new measures to attract more people in the community to the centre. In your report you should explain what new activities and measures have been introduced, such as pricing, opening times, activities for different age groups etc, and how they have affected membership of the centre.

Write your **report**.

3 Your school or university magazine is running a series of articles on how film and/or TV can influence attitudes. Write an article for the magazine briefly describing an appropriate film and/or TV programme and explain to what extent your own attitudes have been influenced by it.

Write your **article**.

4 A prominent news magazine has published an article about the increasing problem of cyberbullying, which means using the internet and online social networks to attack, humiliate and spread lies about other people. Write a letter to the editor of the magazine in response to the article, giving your views on the seriousness of the problem. You should use your own experience or observations to justify your opinion, and make some suggestions as to what could be done to make cyberbullying less common.

Write your **letter**.

Paper 3 – Listening (approx. 40 minutes)

Part 1

You will hear three different extracts. For questions **1-6**, choose the answer (**A**, **B** or **C**) which fits best according to what you hear. There are two questions for each extract.

Extract One

You hear a husband and wife talking about their child's education.

1   The couple agree

    A   on their son's ability to make good decisions.

    B   that their son should be self-sufficient.

    C   on their son's need for formal qualifications.

2   Compared to the man, the woman is

    A   conservative.

    B   ignorant.

    C   realistic.

Extract Two

You hear a specialist discussing colour blindness.

3   Total colour blindness

    A   is more common in men than in women.

    B   is a hereditary condition.

    C   affects fewer people than partial colour blindness.

4   Colour blindness

    A   can exclude the sufferer from some types of employment.

    B   affects many aspects of the sufferer's life.

    C   means sufferers are obliged to undergo tests.

Extract Three

You hear part of a lecture by a sociologist.

5 According to the lecture many people left their homes due to

   A the large number of roads and railways.

   B their inability to find work.

   C the lack of land available.

6 The speaker believes that people's attitudes to work were based on

   A their backgrounds.

   B a desire for profit.

   C market forces.

Part 2

You will hear a radio report about sharks. For questions **7-15**, complete the sentences with a word or short phrase.

In order to film the sharks, Ralf Kiefer had to sit in a [_____ **7** _____] boat near

Seal Island.

Sharks need deep water to give them [_____ **8**] to attack a seal.

Jumping out of the water is possibly a way of [_____ **9**] seals.

Sharks turn over when they breach because their [_____ **10**] at the front.

Sharks have been [_____ **11**] the same for millions of years.

The number of sharks has [_____ **12**] enormously recently.

The shark's [_____ **13**] is a prized ingredient for certain dishes.

A shark produces very few young when it [_____ **14**] .

We should learn to regard sharks as [_____ **15**] that require help to survive.

Part 3

You will hear an interview with Marion D'Souza about homes exchanged for holidays.
For questions **16-20**, choose the answer (**A, B, C** or **D**) which fits best according to what you hear.

16   Marion feels that 'Houseswaps UK' provides safeguards

    A   by its mere existence.

    B   by carefully vetting its clients.

    C   by finding out about a client's home.

    D   by checking available accommodation.

17   Subscription charges are not considered to be too high because

    A   subscribers do not have to pay for the exchange.

    B   of the cost of keeping records up to date.

    C   damage insurance is included in the price.

    D   they issue three catalogues per year.

18   Marion believes that the areas visited will gain because

    A   people will spend more money on accommodation.

    B   families generally prefer home exchanges.

    C   people will have more money to spend when on holiday.

    D   home exchanges are popular with professional people.

19   Marion says that Ana from Spain was

    A   extremely envious.

    B   always enthusiastic.

    C   never satisfied.

    D   initially dubious.

20   Marion thinks that the prospects for 'Houseswaps' are

    A   getting better all the time.

    B   not very good in Spain.

    C   better in Europe than elsewhere.

    D   poor in tourist areas.

Part 4

You will hear five short extracts in which people talk about a disability or medical condition they have.

Task One

For questions **21-25** choose from the list (**A-H**) what challenge each speaker faced due to their condition.

Task Two

For questions **26-30** choose from the list (**A-H**) how their condition caused each speaker to change.

You will hear the recording twice. While you listen, you must complete both tasks.

A   a negative social stigma

B   condescending treatment from others

C   being confined at home

D   embarrassment in front of others

E   a lack of respect at work

F   anxiety about the future

G   misunderstanding social interactions

H   feelings of hopelessness

Speaker 1	21
Speaker 2	22
Speaker 3	23
Speaker 4	24
Speaker 5	25

A   became dependent on a device

B   gave up an activity

C   learned to clarify their behaviour to others

D   became estranged from friends

E   developed a forceful personality

F   cultivated new talents

G   became extremely self-conscious

H   came to accept others curiosity

Speaker 1	26
Speaker 2	27
Speaker 3	28
Speaker 4	29
Speaker 5	30

Paper 4 – Speaking (approx. 16 minutes)

The speaking test involves two candidates and two examiners. One examiner, the Interlocutor, will speak to you while the other, the Assessor, will just listen.

Part 1 (2 minutes)

You will be asked questions in turn about where you live and where you are from, your work, studies and interests, and your views on certain things.

Part 2 (4 minutes)

You will be asked to discuss the photographs on page **131** together. There are two stages in this part.

Stage 1
Here are some photographs of different types of technological advances. Look at pictures 1 and 3 on page 131 and talk together about what life was like before these existed.

Stage 2
Now look at all the pictures. Imagine you are a member of a government committee appointed to invest money in one of the aspects of progress shown. Talk together about which would be the best investment and why the others would be less advantageous.

Part 3 (10 minutes)

You will be asked to talk on your own, comment on what your partner says and join in a three-way discussion with your partner and the Interlocutor around a certain theme.

Work and the workplace

Candidate A will be asked to look at **prompt card (a)** and talk about it for two minutes.
There are also some ideas on the card to use, if the candidate wishes.

Prompt Card (a)
How do you think the workplace will change in the next 50 years?
– working week – robotics – gender roles

Candidate B will then be given **prompt card (b)** and asked to discuss it for two minutes.
There are also some ideas on the card to use, if the candidate wishes.

Prompt Card (b)
To what extent do you think people are fairly paid for the jobs they do?
– athletes/entertainers – the developing world – qualifications

Candidate B will then be asked a question related to the topic:
- *Will people work and shop from home in the future?*

Then the Interlocutor will invite Candidate A to join in using the following prompt:
- *How about you?*

Candidate A will then be asked a question related to the topic:
- *Do athletes and entertainers deserve their high pay?*

Then the Interlocutor will invite Candidate B to join in using the following prompt:
- *What do you think?*

The test will then be concluded with a number of general questions about the topic:
- *Should people be free to cross international borders in search of employment?*
- *To what extent should the state provide employment for people who have been made redundant?*
- *Should the state provide pensions for all?*
- *How great a threat is unemployment?*

Paper 1 – Reading & Use of English *(1 hour 30 minutes)*

Part 1

For questions **1-8**, read the text below and decide which answer (**A**, **B**, **C** or **D**) best fits each gap. Mark your answers **on the separate answer sheet**.

There is an example at the beginning (**0**).

0 **A** influential **B** leading **C** weighty **D** momentous

0	A	B	C	D
	■	□	□	□

Michael Faraday

Michael Faraday was one of the most **(0)** ......A.. scientists in the entire history of science. One of his inventions, a dynamo, is regarded as a **(1)** .... of modern power genenerators. Despite having little in the way of formal education, Faraday was a **(2)** .... reader and autodidact and soon **(3)** .... to the attention of the scientific establishment. He first set **(4)** .... on the path of his professional life as assistant to the renowned scientist Sir Humphrey Davy. Although working for Sir Davy brought Faraday into **(5)** .... with many scientists, he also had to endure class discrimination and was regarded as little more than a servant by the Davy family. It was perhaps due to their mistreatment that Faraday rejected the offer of the presidency of the Royal Society out of **(6)** .... in later life.

Apart from his scientific breakthroughs, Faraday was involved in many projects for the British government. One of the projects he **(7)** .... was to investigate coal mine explosions. Unfortunately, the government **(8)** .... his report inconclusive and it was to be another 60 years before his warnings were heeded.

1	**A**	vanguard	**B**	envoy	**C**	herald	**D**	forerunner
2	**A**	singular	**B**	prodigious	**C**	remarkable	**D**	talented
3	**A**	stood	**B**	fell	**C**	brought	**D**	came
4	**A**	forth	**B**	ahead	**C**	before	**D**	forward
5	**A**	connection	**B**	association	**C**	contact	**D**	acquaintance
6	**A**	hand	**B**	mind	**C**	touch	**D**	reason
7	**A**	terminated	**B**	finalised	**C**	contracted	**D**	undertook
8	**A**	assessed	**B**	deemed	**C**	concluded	**D**	rated

Part 2

For questions **9-16**, read the text below and think of the word which best fits each space. Use only **one** word in each space. There is an example at the beginning (0). Write your answers **IN CAPITAL LETTERS on the separate answer sheet**.

Example: | 0 | I | T | S | E | L | F | | | | | | | | | |

Defining Work

Work has always been a central focus point for society, but as old as the idea of work (0) ....ITSELF.... is the question of what constitutes 'real work'. (9) .... you to ask a miner what real work is, he'd probably reply that it entails working with your hands. To the average blue collar worker, white collar workers are the people who sit in offices day (10) .... day doing little or (11) .... in the line of actual work. If you approached a white collar worker or professional of (12) .... sort with the same question, you can rest assured they'd adamantly maintain that the world would stop revolving (13) .... their invaluable intellectual contribution.

It's also illuminating to look at the vocabulary used to describe work and its related subjects. Words (14) .... career, vocation and profession carry a more elevated connotation than the simple term 'job'. The (15) .... three lexical items convey the idea of educated people sitting at desks and using their grey matter on such things as financial, legal or medical matters, (16) .... the latter one denotes the humble slaving away at some mundane task.

Part 3

For questions **17-24**, read the text below. Use the word given in capitals at the end of some of the lines to form a word that fits in the space in the same line. There is an example at the beginning **(0)**. Write your answers **IN CAPITAL LETTERS on the separate answer sheet.**

Example:

0	C	O	M	P	O	S	I	T	I	O	N	S						

Lloyd Webber Musicals

Andrew Lloyd Webber, whose rock based **(0)** ..COMPOSITIONS.. helped   **COMPOSE**

(17) .... English musical theatre in the late 20th century,   **VITAL**

began his career while still at Oxford University. It was there that he formed a

(18) .... with Timothy Rice and they began putting on   **PARTNER**

productions.

Their first **(19)** .... successful venture was *Joseph and the*   **NOTE**

Amazing Technicolour Dreamcoat, a children's pop oratorio that earned world-

wide **(20)** .... Then came the rock opera *Jesus Christ*   **CLAIM**

Superstar, a controversial look at Jesus's life story that became one of the

longest running shows in British **(21)** .... history. *Evita* was   **THEATRE**

Lloyd Webber's final collaboration with Rice and for his next production, *Cats*,

he used two **(22)** ...., Hart and Stilgoe. He then   **LYRIC**

composed a hugely successful version of *Phantom of the Opera*.

Lloyd Webber's productions have always been flashy spectacles and much of

his success is due to his ability to blend such varied and **(23)** ....   **SIMILAR**

genres as rock and roll, English music hall song and **(24)** ....   **OPERA**

forms into music with a wide mass appeal.

Part 4

For questions **25-30**, complete the second sentence so that it has a similar meaning to the first sentence, using the word given. **Do not change the word given.** You must use between **three** and **eight** words, including the word given. Here is an example (**0**).

Example:

0   We are able to afford a holiday, because I was promoted.

   result

   As ...., we are able to afford a holiday.

0	*a result of my promotion*

Write **only** the missing words **on the separate answer sheet.**

---

25   The council is unlikely to approve the plans for a new sports centre unless the cost is reduced.

   meet

   The plans for a new sports centre are ....
   unless the cost is reduced.

26   Lack of adequate collateral may mean that the bank will have to refuse his loan.

   impossible

   Lack of adequate collateral may .... him a
   loan.

27   I will see to it that the goods are delivered immediately.

arrange

I will .... the goods.

28   You must remember to pay the phone bill today whatever you do.

account

On .... to pay the phone bill today.

29   The owner's mismanagement was directly responsible for the company failing to succeed.

consequence

The company's .... the owner's mismanagement.

30   He said he had nothing to do with causing the accident.

blame

He refused to .... the accident.

Part 5

You are going to read an extract from an article about advertising aimed at children. For questions **31-36**, choose the answer (**A**, **B**, **C** or **D**) which you think fits best according to the text. Mark your answers **on the separate answer sheet**.

Advertising Shifts Focus

The average citizen is bombarded with TV commercials, posters and newspaper advertisements wherever he goes. Not only this, but promotional material is constantly on view, with every available public space from shop to petrol station covered with advertising of some kind. People who are foolish enough to drive with their windows open are likely to have leaflets advertising everything and anything thrust in at them. The amount of advertising to which we are exposed is phenomenal, yet advertisers are being hurt by their industry's worst recession in a decade and a conviction that is in many respects more frightening than the booms and busts of capitalism: the belief that advertising can go no further. Despite the ingenuity of the advertisers, who, in their need to make their advertisements as visually attractive as possible, often totally obscure the message, the consumer has become increasingly cynical and simply blanks out all but the subtlest messages. The advertising industry has therefore turned to a more vulnerable target: the young.

The messages specifically aimed at children are for toys and games – whose promotional budgets increased fivefold in the 1990s – and fast food, which dominates the children's advertising market. However, the main thrust of advertising in this area is no longer towards traditional children's products. Advertisers acknowledge that the commercial pressures of the 1990s had an extraordinary effect on childhood: it is now generally believed that the cut-off point for buying toys has been falling by one year every five years. Research suggests that while not so many years ago children were happy with Lego or similar construction games at ten or eleven, most of today's children abandon them at six or seven. In effect, the result is the premature ageing of children.

There is nowhere where the advertising industry's latest preoccupation with the young is so evident as in schools. Increasingly low budgets have left schools vulnerable to corporate funding and sponsorship schemes in order to provide much needed equipment, such as computers, or to enable them to run literacy schemes. While on the face of it this would seem to be a purely philanthropic gesture on the part of the companies concerned, the other side of the coin is a pervasive commercial presence in the classroom, where textbooks and resource books are increasingly likely to bear a company logo.

This marked shift in advertising perceptions also means that a great deal of supposedly adult advertising has an infantile appeal, inasmuch as adult products can be presented within an anecdote or narrative, thus making the message more accessible to young teenagers and smaller children. Children obviously cannot buy these things for themselves; what is behind these advertisements is more subtle. Advertisers have come to recognize that if children can successfully pester their parents to buy them the latest line in trainers, then they can also influence their parent's choice of car or credit card, and so children become an advertising tool in themselves.

There are many, on all sides of the ideological spectrum, who would argue that advertising has little influence on children, who are exposed to such a huge variety of visual images that advertisements simply become lost in the crowd. Rather, they would argue that it is the indulgent parents, who do not wish their children to lack for anything, who boost sales figures. While there may be a great deal of truth in this, it would seem that to deny that advertising influences at all because there is so much of it, while accepting that other aspects of life do have an effect, is a little disingenuous. In fact, the advertising industry itself admits that since peer pressure plays such an important role in children's lives, they are not difficult to persuade. And of course, their minds are not yet subject to the advertising overload their parents suffer from. The question that arises is whether indeed we as a society can accept that children, far from being in some sense protected from the myriad of pressures, decisions and choices which impinge on an adult's life, should now be exposed to this influence in all aspects of their lives, in ways that we as adults have no control over. Or do we take the attitude that, as with everything else from crossing city streets to the intense competition of the modern world, children will have to learn to cope, so the sooner they are exposed the better?

31   What does the writer say about advertising in the first paragraph?

   A   Capitalism has led to the demise of advertising.
   B   We should have a cynical view of advertisers.
   C   Advertising is facing new challenges these days.
   D   The industry has run out of new ideas.

32   The bombardment of advertisements has led to

   A   children taking more notice of them.
   B   greater difficulty in attracting consumers' attention.
   C   more appealing advertisements.
   D   people being less likely to spend money.

33   How have children changed during the past decade?

   A   They have become consumers.
   B   They are growing up more quickly.
   C   They are becoming cleverer.
   D   They are not playing as much.

34   What does the writer imply in the third paragraph?

   A   Advertising agencies need to preserve their reputations.
   B   Schools welcome aid from big business.
   C   There are restrictions on how financial aid may be used.
   D   Companies expect nothing in return for their help.

35   How have children changed the face of advertising?

   A   Children are influencing the purchases of adult products.
   B   They are now the advertising industry's sole market.
   C   More products have to be sold to children.
   D   Children have become more selective in their choices.

36   The writer's purpose is to

   A   explain the inspiration for advertisements.
   B   expose the exploitation of children.
   C   deter parents from giving in to advertisers.
   D   prevent advertisers from infiltrating schools.

Part 6

You are going to read an article about the Bradshaw rock paintings. Seven paragraphs have been removed from the extract. Choose from the paragraphs **A-H** the one which fits each gap (**37-43**). There is one extra paragraph which you do not need to use. **Mark your answers on the separate answer sheet**.

Spellbound

All eyes are on the shaman: arms outstretched, head back, her face hidden behind a mask. She wears a long, tapering cap, and clutches a short wand in each hand. There are tassels at her hips and elbows, and these jump as she begins to move. The crowd around her watches, spellbound, as she embarks upon her journey to the spirit world.

37

The suggestion that this rock art may be the oldest known depiction of a shamanistic ritual comes from a group of researchers led by Per Michaelsen, a geologist at James Cook University in Queensland. They argue that these ancient paintings may represent not only early religious practices but perhaps also a cultural heritage common to all humans. Such daring new theories do not go down well with the rock art establishment. But regardless of which ideas prevail, the controversy is certain to attract attention to an astonishing record of a vanished people.

38

Michaelsen estimates that there may be as many as 100,000 Bradshaw 'galleries' tucked under rock overhangs along the region's major river systems. Many of the paintings have never been studied. But observations made by other researchers over the past few decades reveal several distinct artistic styles. Researchers recognise at least four major periods which they can place in chronological order by looking at patterns of weathering and instances where one style is superimposed upon another.

39

The subjects' dress changes over time, as does the style of the paintings themselves. The next oldest figures are notable for the sashes around their midriffs. These sash figures still have armbands, but not the prominent tassels.

40

There are also so-called elegant action figures of people running and hunting, which are difficult to date because none is superimposed on a painting from another period. However, the abstract style suggests that they were created some time after the tassel and sash figures.

41

In 1997, a group led by Richard Roberts, now at the University of Melbourne, used a technique known as luminescence dating to assign a minimum age of 17,000 years to one of the younger paintings. The second study, also published in 1997, used radiocarbon dating and came up with a much younger estimate: about 4,000 years. Its author, Alan Watchman, believes the Bradshaw culture might date back from between 5,000 and 6,000 years, but rejects the idea that it could be 17,000 years old or more.

42

Either way, the Bradshaw people were not the original inhabitants of the Kimberley. Their paintings have little in common with the crudely rendered animals of the region's oldest art. Archaeological evidence suggests the first settlers of the Kimberley arrived at least 40,000 years ago. They would have found a region of open tropical forest and woodlands where they seem to have flourished for 10,000 years. Then things began to change.

43

Intriguingly, one of the Bradshaw paintings shows a boat with upswept prow and stern, and multiple paddlers. It raises the possibility that the artists were originally a seafaring people. The idea that the Bradshaw people came from Indonesia or further afield has a long pedigree in Australian anthropology, but there is no hard evidence to support it.

A Both researchers stand by their results. Roberts suspects that Watchman's radiocarbon samples might have been contaminated by traces of younger carbon. Watchman thinks that the painting dated by Roberts was, in fact, pre-Bradshaw. Despite their differences of opinion, the two are currently working together and expect to present new results before the end of the year.

B The Bradshaws, as the paintings are collectively known, were first noted by Europeans in 1891 and take their name from Joseph Bradshaw, the rancher who described them. They are found in a region known as the Kimberley, a remote place even by Australian standards. It is a rugged sandstone landscape of plunging canyons and treacherous swamps.

C Younger than the sash and tasselled figures, the clothes-peg figures are much more highly stylised. The older paintings tend to show profiles, but these are frontal portraits. Gone is the anatomical detail, and many figures assume aggressive stances and carry multi-barbed spears and spear throwers.

D The Ice Age brought cooler temperatures, strong winds and lower rainfall to northern Australia. The sea level dropped, and at times, during the glacial maximum, it was up to 140 metres below its present level. The coastline was as much as 400 kilometres further to the north-west. Australia was connected by land to New Guinea and separated from Southeast Asia by just a narrow channel. Could the Bradshaw culture have arrived in Australia at this time?

E The others are sceptical. Grahame Walsh, author of the most comprehensive book on the Bradshaws to date, is critical of the newcomers' lack of experience. He says that there are many people beginning to enter the Kimberley rock art scene and set themselves up as experts. He has so far found nothing that indicates shamanism and warns that one has to be extremely cautious in attempting to link such prehistoric art with comparatively modern art in distant countries.

F All these paintings provide a wealth of detail about the material culture of the Bradshaw people. Yet, despite this, nobody knows when the Bradshaw culture developed or where it came from. Only two groups have attempted to date the paintings directly, and their results are widely different.

G The oldest and largest paintings, which are up to 1.7 metres tall, are known as the tasselled figures. They are the most realistic of the images and show figures in static poses in what appears to be ceremonial dress. The figures are characterised by tassels attached to the upper arms, elbows, hips and knees.

H That is one possible interpretation of a scene recorded thousands of years ago on a remote rocky outcrop in north-west Australia. The painting is part of a vast collection that opens a window on an ancient, hunter-gatherer society that may date back to the last ice age. Despite the quality and extent of this record, much about the paintings remains a mystery. Who were the artists? When were the paintings done – and what do they mean?

Part 7

You are going to read extracts related to precious stones.
For questions **44-53**, choose from the sections (**A-E**). The sections may be chosen more than once.

Mark your answers **on the separate answer sheet**.

In which section are the following mentioned?

assembling treasures in order to enhance the status of the monarchy	**44** ....
the possibility of making semi-precious jewels popular	**45** ....
the accidental discovery of a valuable jewel	**46** ....
the success of a devious business tactic	**47** ....
conjecture about the fate of a large number of jewels	**48** ....
the link between a business and the public's attitude to close relationships	**49** ....
the variety of a manufactured gemstone	**50** ....
information on how a rewarding relationship began	**51** ....
the chemical composition of a type of gem	**52** ....
the devastating effect of an activity on the environment	**53** ....

Precious Stones

A What is a Diamond?

Diamond, like graphite and charcoal, is a form of carbon. It crystallises in cubic form, at enormous pressures and high temperatures over the course of millions of years. The process has been imitated under laboratory conditions to create artificial diamonds. These have proven to be mainly of either industrial use, plain quality or very small in size. The diamond's exceptional properties arise from its structure, in which the bonding between the carbon atoms is immensely strong and uniform.

A diamond possesses extraordinary powers of light reflection. When properly cut, it gathers light within itself, reflecting it back in a shower of fire and brilliance. Second, it is the only gem mineral composed of a single, unadulterated element, making it the purest of earth's gemstones. Thirdly, it is the hardest transparent substance known to man. The only material that can cut diamond is ... another diamond!

B An Unusual Stone

In the latter part of the 19th century, the jewellery profession was strictly confined to precious stones. No so-called fancy stones were on sale in any jewellery store in the country; yet, reviewing the beautiful minerals that I had gathered, it seemed to me that many women would be happy to array themselves in the endless gorgeous colours of these gems. So one day, I wrapped a tourmaline in a bit of gem paper, and all the way to my destination rehearsed my arguments. I was received by the managing head of what was, even then, the largest jewellery establishment in the world and showed him my drop of green light. I explained – very little; the gem itself was its own best argument. Tiffany bought it – the great dealers in precious stones bought their first tourmaline from me. I had interested the foremost jeweller of that time in my revolutionary theory and made the acquaintance of a man who was later to become my close friend.

C Diamonds are a Girl's Best Friend

'Diamonds are a girl's best friend,' professed Marilyn Monroe. Composed of pure carbon, the rock is not the rarest of gems but found in abundance the world over. However, every time one is purchased, a credulous public is buying into a cunning marketing campaign conceived by the De Beers' cartel – a company that almost since its beginning in the late 19th century has attempted to control the world's diamond supply.

After the Great Depression, Sir Ernest Oppenheimer needed another market for his wares. The objective was to transform America's taste for small low-quality stones into one which would open its wallets to higher-quality gems.

Into the hands of the N. W. Ayer advertising agency came the challenge. The American attitudes towards gift giving and romance were researched extensively, resulting in an enduring advertising campaign. Without ever mentioning the De Beers name, 'A Diamond is Forever' was the slogan used to establish a tradition aimed at capturing hearts and loosening purse strings. Diamond rings became the best way to declare one's eternal love. The bigger the rock, the greater the devotion. Furthermore, one's salary could be ostentatiously flaunted on a woman's finger.

D Jade

As the sun's first glow appears, its aura illuminates a Yunnan trader preparing for the day ahead. With a watchmaker's precision, all the possessions in his earthly world are gathered together and placed into burlap sacks. These are then strapped onto a mule's saddle, a stone picked up from the nearby river helping to balance the load.

He sets off in the misty light just before dawn, the surrounding jungle pushes in everywhere, each step a mark of patience – down the track, into the sunlight... into history... into immortality... for the rock on the mule's back is no ordinary stone. Burma's jade mines are on the brink of discovery.

In the same remote corner of the planet, yesteryear's idyll is today broken. Across the naked earth crawl thousands of human ants, prying boulders loose from the compact brown soil. They are quickly examined, then discarded. The operation is a study in patience. The construction of Egypt's Great Pyramids was a similar study in patience but with one important difference. That in Upper Burma consists of deconstruction, the dismantling of entire mountains, one pebble at a time.

E The State Diamond Fund

In 1719, The Emperor Peter I, Peter The Great, created a permanent fund to house a collection of Royal Romanov jewels that were to be bequeathed to the state by each successive ruler. The State Diamond Fund was to collect jewels under the condition that they could not be altered, sold or given away and that the collection was to be for the glory of the Russian Empire.

The collection was originally housed in the Diamond Chamber in the Winter Palace. Peter started the fund with a donation of jewellery, including the pieces used in his coronation ceremony. Each subsequent monarch then went on to donate additions to the collection until the end of the Romanov Dynasty during the Russian revolution. What happened to the full collection after that is a matter of speculation. Many pieces are said to have been looted during the upheaval of the early days of the Soviet state and still more sold. But the remnants of the collection are on permanent display at the Kremlin museum.

Paper 2 – Writing *(1 hour 30 mins)*

Part 1

Read the two texts below.

Write an essay summarising and evaluating the key points from both texts. Use your own words throughout as far as possible, and include your own ideas in your answers.

Write your answer in **240-280 words on the separate answer sheet**.

1

Childhood Dyslexia

Dyslexia can affect much more than the child's ability to read. There may be difficulties in problem solving, concentration or remembering pieces of information. If the children are allowed to work at their own pace and level, then results can be achieved. But if the condition is not picked up, it is not unusual for the dyslexic child to find that school is a particularly hostile environment, since the child is all too often labelled, by peers and teachers alike, as simply lazy or of low intelligence. It is vital that teachers be aware of dyslexia and provide a secure classroom environment.

Adult Dyslexia

If an adult is assessed as dyslexic, a report would then provide a full description of the individual's strengths and weaknesses with recommendations for action, such as applying for support on courses or within the workplace. Experience suggests that the majority of dyslexic adults are relieved to discover their dyslexia. It enables them to understand their educational history and put past experiences into context. This relieves some of the frustration they will inevitably have felt. When dyslexic adults understand their dyslexia, they are able to continue in education. In a sympathetic environment dyslexic adults can fulfill their potential and improve their skills effectively.

Write your **essay**.

Part 2

Write an answer to **one** of the questions **2-4** in this part. Write your answer in **280-320** words in an appropriate style **on the separate answer sheet**. Put the question number in the box at the top of the answer sheet.

2   A magazine has asked its readers to contribute to a special edition it is bringing out entitled *Childhood to Adulthood*. Readers are invited to send in articles in which they describe childhood experiences which had a great influence on their lives.

   Write your **article**.

3   You work for the newly set up local tourist board of a previously undeveloped part of your country. The board is trying to promote the area as a destination for summer and winter holidays. You have been asked to visit some local places of interest to assess their value in attracting tourists and to write a report with your findings.

   Write your **report**.

4   A new branch of a trendy upmarket restaurant has just opened in your town. You recently visited the restaurant with a friend. You decide to send the local newspaper a review describing the food, decor, service and price and explaining why you would or would not recommend the restaurant to locals.

   Write your **review**.

Paper 3 – Listening (*approx. 40 minutes*)

Part 1

You will hear three different extracts. For questions **1-6**, choose the answer (**A**, **B** or **C**) which fits best according to what you hear. There are two questions for each extract.

Extract One

You hear two marriage guidance counsellors talking about quarrelling.

1 The couple

    A   agree the husband has had a stressful day.

    B   agree his wife is a bad cook.

    C   can't agree on financial matters.

2 Quarrelling

    A   is often prevented early.

    B   leads to further bitterness.

    C   can be humorous.

Extract Two

You hear a historian talking about the Fire of London.

3 The speaker says that the fire was

    A   set deliberately.

    B   hampered by high winds.

    C   put out twice.

4 The speaker comments that as a result of the fire

    A   the layout of London's streets was radically changed.

    B   St. Paul's Cathedral was built as a memorial.

    C   a large edifice now stands near to where the fire began.

Extract Three

You hear part of an advertisement for a sports facility.

5   According to the speaker, the Angus South Course

   A   caters for professional golfers.

   B   has knowledgeable employees.

   C   has changed its name.

6   The speaker feels that

   A   both courses are well-designed.

   B   each course caters for different skills.

   C   both courses have been extremely successful.

Part 2

You will hear a part of a radio talk on an ancient Mesoamerican city and the discoveries that were made there. For questions **7-15**, complete the sentences with a word or short phrase.

The Aztecs believed that Teotihuacán had been constructed by [_____ 7] .

Teotihuacán [_____ 8] was bigger than many other

ancient cities.

Our inability to read the [_____ 9] limits our

knowledge of how people lived in the city.

Bones discovered in 1989 seem to have belonged to [_____ 10]

buried with their weapons.

The archeologist compares the construction of Mesoamerican pyramids to that of an

[_____ 11] .

The way the pyramids were built makes it [_____ 12]

to gain access to the central room.

The objects discovered make this the most important [_____ 13]

found at Teotihuacán.

If the skeleton had sharpened teeth and precious jewellery, this would indicate [_____ 14] .

In order to shed more light on the city and its civilization, further

[_____ 15] must be done.

Part 3

You will hear an interview with Jack Taylor, the creator of the very popular cartoon character, Carla. For questions **16-20**, choose the answer (**A**, **B**, **C** or **D**) which fits best according to what you hear.

16   Jack is bemused by his character's popularity because

   A   he never thought Carla would be attractive to adults.

   B   crocodiles aren't particularly loveable.

   C   Carla has drawn so many families closer together.

   D   Carla is rather old.

17   According to Jack, Carla's character

   A   came to him, as he was reading to his child.

   B   developed slowly over a period of time.

   C   was meant to cheer up his recuperating daughter.

   D   was meant to mirror an actual person.

18   According to Jack, Carla

   A   made him wealthy when she first appeared.

   B   has appeared in children's theatre.

   C   is still important in his daughter's life.

   D   was so popular that he continued creating stories.

19   Carla's recent rise to fame came about

   A   when adults started enjoying the stories.

   B   after her TV show was broadcast in foreign countries.

   C   following a meeting with a producer after an event.

   D   because of marketing in the run-up to Christmas.

20   Jack believes that his books

   A   have benefited from the merchandising.

   B   are less important than the TV programme.

   C   only appeal to girls.

   D   have been exploited for commercial reasons.

Part 4

You will hear five short extracts in which people talk about the role technology plays in their life.

Task One
For questions **21-25** choose from the list (**A-H**) what each speaker wants from technology.

Task Two
For questions **26-30** choose from the list (**A-H**) what each speaker has come to believe about technology.

You will hear the recording twice. While you listen, you must complete both tasks.

A	an interesting diversion		
B	educational opportunities	Speaker 1	21
C	as little as possible	Speaker 2	22
D	expansion of business opportunities	Speaker 3	23
E	a connection with loved ones	Speaker 4	24
		Speaker 5	25
F	improved health and safety		
G	increased self-reliance		
H	enhanced popularity		

A	Innovation is not decreasing.		
B	Greed is the driving force.	Speaker 1	26
C	It is fun for all ages.	Speaker 2	27
D	It is for a younger generation.	Speaker 3	28
E	It is not just harmless fun.	Speaker 4	29
		Speaker 5	30
F	It is a violation of privacy.		
G	It is accessible to novices.		
H	It can not solve every problem.		

Paper 4 – Speaking *(approx. 16 minutes)*

The speaking test involves two candidates and two examiners. One examiner, the Interlocutor, will speak to you while the other, the Assessor, will just listen.

Part 1 *(2 minutes)*

You will be asked questions in turn about where you live and where you are from, your work, studies and interests, and your views on certain things.

Part 2 *(4 minutes)*

You will be asked to discuss the photographs on page **132** together. There are two stages in this part.

Stage 1
Here are some photographs which show the way in which today's young people express themselves. Look at photographs 1 and 2 on page 132 and discuss how the images relate to the lifestyle of young people today.

Stage 2
Now look at all the pictures. Imagine these photographs are being used by parents' groups to demonstrate to the authorities the need for more facilities and activities for the youth of your town. Discuss what each image shows and talk about how young people's energies can be channelled in a positive way.

Part 3 *(10 minutes)*

You will be asked to talk on your own, comment on what your partner says and join in a three-way discussion with your partner and the Interlocutor around a particular theme.

Fashion

Candidate A will be asked to look at **prompt card (a)** and talk about it for two minutes.
There are also some ideas on the card to use, if the candidate wishes.

Candidate B will then be given **prompt card (b)** and asked to discuss it for two minutes.
There are also some ideas on the card to use, if the candidate wishes.

Prompt Card (a)
Can you judge a person by what they wear?
– first impressions – dress code – money

Prompt Card (b)
Is modern life more demanding than it used to be?
– fear of rejection – peer pressure – image enhancement

Candidate B will then be asked a question related to the topic:
- *How do people express themselves by what they wear?*

Then the Interlocutor will invite Candidate A to join in using the following prompt:
- *What do you think?*

Candidate A will then be asked a question related to the topic:
- *Does the media influence the way young people behave nowadays?*

Then the Interlocutor will invite Candidate B to join in using the following prompt:
- *What is your view?*

The test will then be concluded with a number of general questions about the topic:

- *How does the media influence our ideas on fashion?*
- *Has society got the right to dictate what people wear?*
- *In what other areas of life does fashion play a role?*
- *How far do you think people should be followers of fashion?*

Paper 1 – Reading & Use of English *(1 hour 30 minutes)*

Part 1

For questions **1-8**, read the text below and decide which answer (**A**, **B**, **C** or **D**) best fits each gap. Mark your answers **on the separate answer sheet**.

There is an example at the beginning (**0**).

0   **A**   priceless   **B**   precious   **C**   cherished   **D**   extortionate

0	A	B	C	D
	☐	▆	☐	☐

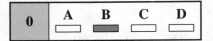

Gold

Almost every culture in the world has valued gold in its various forms and sought it as a **(0)** .....B..... metal, either to worship or to trade in. A symbol of power and success, the desire to own it tends to provoke both greed and lust. Its very presence can make or **(1)** .... a nation. The esteem associated with it has driven mankind to great **(2)** .... to obtain it. And the great gold **(3)** .... of the 19th century saw hundreds of thousands die in an attempt to **(4)** .... it rich. Despite declining gold prices and uncertainties in the market, as countries such as Australia and Britain sell off large portions of their gold **(5)** ...., the desire to find gold is as strong as ever. In the US, **(6)** .... for gold has become a huge leisure industry, where once men **(7)** .... and slaved for the glitter of gold, families now go out for a picnic while looking for gold. However, for most, it is still only the **(8)** .... of dreams.

1	**A**	take	**B**	shatter	**C**	break	**D**	crack
2	**A**	spans	**B**	measures	**C**	distances	**D**	lengths
3	**A**	rushes	**B**	dashes	**C**	charges	**D**	stampedes
4	**A**	make	**B**	strike	**C**	get	**D**	land
5	**A**	hoards	**B**	reserves	**C**	markets	**D**	stocks
6	**A**	filtering	**B**	swilling	**C**	panning	**D**	sifting
7	**A**	trudged	**B**	reeked	**C**	preened	**D**	slogged
8	**A**	pipe	**B**	stuff	**C**	froth	**D**	whiff

Part 2

For questions **9-16**, read the text below and think of the word which best fits each space. Use only **one** word in each space. There is an example at the beginning (**0**). Write your answers **IN CAPITAL LETTERS on the separate answer sheet**.

Example: | **0** | B | E | T | W | E | E | N | | | | | | | | | | |

Theatre Design

Built (**0**) .B.E.T.W.E.E.N. 350 and 330 BC, the semi-circular theatre at Epidauros in Greece has (**9**) .... been bettered. Its acoustics are near perfect, its design and natural setting breathtaking. Has theatre design really got anywhere since Epidauros?

In today's world, (**10**) .... remains a divide between the expectations of traditionally-minded audiences and (**11**) .... of inventive theatrical companies, with no one seeming to know quite (**12**) .... a theatre needs to be – a group of wandering players or permanently housed in magnificent buildings?

In the (**13**) .... case, going to see a play is like going to the cinema: actors play on a distant stage framed by heavy curtains. There is (**14**) .... similarity between this and the audience participation promoted by other theatre groups; the two experiences are quite (**15**) .... each other, require different architectural settings and, (**16**) .... date, have appealed to different kinds of audiences.

Part 3

For questions **17-24**, read the text below. Use the word given in capitals at the end of some of the lines to form a word that fits in the space in the same line. There is an example at the beginning **(0)**. Write your answers **IN CAPITAL LETTERS on the separate answer sheet.**

Example: | **0** | A S S I S T A N C E |

With Many Thanks

Many people have given **(0)** ASSISTANCE......... to me during the writing of   **ASSIST**

this book, but it is to Ms Leigh Keith, senior editor of Ramsay and Brown that

I am most deeply **(17)** .... to for her loyalty and   **DEBT**

encouragement during the four years the project lasted. She gave her time

and advice **(18)** .... in order for this work to be completed,   **STINT**

giving both moral and practical support for the lengthy research into social

conditions the project **(19)** .... Her confidence in me   **NECESSARY**

sustained me in my belief that this was valuable work and it was

undoubtedly what **(20)** .... me to continue in the face of   **ABLE**

often discouraging circumstances.

I must also thank my father, who has been a willing **(21)** ....   **COLLABORATE**

in all my efforts and who spent long hours in libraries and on trains to distant

parts of the country in search of material. I know that he will say he enjoyed

it, but without his **(22)** .... enthusiasm this book would   **FLAG**

never have seen the light of day. Finally, I would like to give my friends and

family the **(23)** .... they so richly deserve. They have had to   **RECOGNISE**

put up with what must have seemed to them an **(24)** ....   **EXCEPT**

long drawn out piece of writing. Thank you, all of you, very much.

Part 4

For questions **25-30**, complete the second sentence so that it has a similar meaning to the first sentence, using the word given. **Do not change the word given.** You must use between **three** and **eight** words, including the word given. Here is an example **(0)**.

Example:

0   We are able to afford a holiday, because I was promoted.

    result

    As .... , we are able to afford a holiday.

0	*a result of my promotion*

Write **only** the missing words **on the separate answer sheet.**

---

25   He really wants to become an astronaut.

    intent

    He .... an astronaut.

26   Roger insisted he knew nothing about the recent scandal.

    knowledge

    Roger .... the recent scandal.

27   Her friends still hadn't arrived by 9 o'clock so Helen went to the party alone.

      sign

      There .... 9 o'clock, so Helen went to the party alone.

28   It looks as though John doesn't want to buy that house after all.

      decided

      John seems .... that house after all.

29   She's not very good at arranging flowers.

      flair

      She .... arranging flowers.

30   My salary never lasts beyond the end of the month.

      short

      I .... the end of the month.

Part 5

You are going to read an extract from an autobiography. For questions **31-36**, choose the answer (**A**, **B**, **C** or **D**) which you think fits best according to the text. Mark your answers **on the separate answer sheet**.

Autobiography

It was true I read a lot, but by now I had graduated to adult reading. Dickens had my full attention, for surely in those novels he was telling the same story of travail and triumph. The additional benefit, apart from the eccentric characters with their eccentric names, was that many of these travails were undertaken by young men of peerless disposition. This was welcome proof that such life experiences were universal, and, more important, could be, and usually were, brought about while suffering an initial handicap – wicked step-parents, or an indigent family – which the hero (for David Copperfield and Nicholas Nickleby were undoubted heroes) could manage with little more than his own blamelessness to guide him. This struck me as entirely beautiful and convinced me that one must emulate their efforts, that one must never be discouraged by the unhelpfulness of others. Not that I had ever experienced such an obstacle at close quarters; what I took for wickedness was in fact worldliness, as my mother explained to me.

The unapologetic presence of our visitors, their peculiar blend of restlessness and complacency, which was discordant, was essentially harmless, though it occasionally sought relief in imprecations, in disapproval of others, principally of my mother and myself. I saw – in Nancy's hoarse smoker's laugh, in Millicent's delicate hand smoothing her hair – a quality that was alien to our own lives, faintly undesirable. Sometimes my mother's eyes had a look of tiredness, and she was obliged to turn her head away for a brief moment, as suggestions for improvement, or rather self-improvement, came her way. These visits, which I now see were undertaken for more merciful reasons than mere curiosity, were in essence a form of female solidarity before that condition had been politicised. They were concerned for any woman, living on her own with only a child for company. At the same time, they were fearful that such ivory tower isolation might be catching. They wanted my mother to be reinstated in society for their sakes as much as her own. They genuinely pitied a woman who had no status, but they also translated this lack of status as failure in the world's terms.

What distinguished my mother was a form of guilelessness which they had, regretfully, laid aside. This is what I saw: they had exchanged one position for another and may not have been entirely compensated. My mother was their crusade; they also usefully saw her as a pupil. When they rose to leave, the frowns disappeared from their faces, the concern evaporated, and their embraces were genuine. They were glad to get back to their own orbit, with its comprehensible distractions, glad to have done their social duty, even if the results were so sadly lacking. My mother, shaking cushions after their departure, would be more silent than usual, and I somehow knew I should not intrude on her thoughts. I reflected that Nancy and Millie were characters, no less and no more, and that any confrontation – but none had taken place nor would take place – would be unequal: my mother was bound to succeed, for she was untainted by the world's corruption and thus qualified for remission. I comforted myself that even David Copperfield had had moments of downheartedness.

On the whole, I was happy. I liked my school, I liked my friends; I liked the shabby charm of my flat from which a light shone out in winter to guide me home. I liked our silent streets, the big windows of the houses in which artists had once lived. I liked its emanations of the nineteenth century. That we were somewhat on the margin of things did not disturb me, although the girls making their way by car from Kensington, complained of the distance, as if they had been obliged to cross a frontier, or to go back in time. It is true that our surroundings were a little mournful, perhaps unnaturally so to those habitual shoppers. I, on the other hand, cherished them as a place of safety. The street lamp that shone outside my bedroom window I accepted as a benign gesture on behalf of the town council, the man who swept the leaves in autumn as a guardian of our decency. I was hardly aware of the sound of cars, for fewer people drove then. Even footfalls sounded discreet and distant.

31 What does the writer say about Dickens' novels?

A   She has always found them to be intriguing.

B   They often portrayed hard work and success.

C   They were unequalled by other novels of that time.

D   The main characters were invariably impoverished orphans.

32 The writer's mother seemed to

A   enjoy Nancy and Millicent's visits.

B   disapprove of Nancy and Millicent.

C   tolerate the remarks they made.

D   become visibly angry when they spoke.

33 According to the writer the visitors were

A   persistently critical.

B   extremely sensitive.

C   fundamentally supportive.

D   utterly contemptuous.

34 In paragraph 3, how does the writer react after the visitors leave?

A   She feels happy the visit was brief.

B   She tries to lift her mother's spirits.

C   She hopes they will not visit again.

D   She reflects that others have felt the same.

35 To the writer, her neighbourhood is

A   a place where artists gather.

B   too far away from her friends.

C   a refuge from the world.

D   a depressing, rundown area.

36 The writer gives the impression of having been

A   always happy during childhood.

B   blessed with an exceptionally thrilling childhood.

C   protected from the outside world.

D   thankful to have overcome life's hardships.

Part 6

You are going to read an extract from a novel. Seven paragraphs have been removed from the extract. Choose from the paragraphs **A-H** the one which fits each gap **(37-43)**. There is one extra paragraph which you do not need to use. **Mark your answers on the separate answer sheet**.

A Pioneering Study

When Booth conducted his survey, he had no precedents to guide him except occasional reports from factory inspectors, royal commissions, the census and other statistical surveys. There had been no inquiry into poverty in general, no breakdown of income and classes. In attempting to deal with just these problems through his own observations, Booth, despite the defects of his methods, was a pioneer.

37

There is an openness to reality, a willingness to look at squalor without coating it over with moralistic language, and a humility before the plight of some of the poor, which give the writing a literary distinctiveness truly reminiscent of Orwell's own efforts to assert decency. It is journalistic without seeming callous and sensationalist. 'Here in Ferdinand Street,' he writes of one packed block of houses, 'not an inch was lost, and the fingers of any one passer-by might have tapped at any window or door as he passed along.'

38

He has a remarkably good ear for common speech and an eye for telling details. One pictures him tall, stooped, notebook in hand, intent upon his subject, asking frequent questions, at times a trifle self-deprecating, but never so aware of his posture as to lose sight of his inquiry. Booth was, apparently, courteous almost to a fault, and his prose is a perfectly unaffected vehicle for such decorum. Sometimes we are hardly conscious of the intrusion of his style.

39

Whether Booth's manner, which lends so much dignity to the poor without special pleading, would be as appropriate to writing about them today is worth considering. Nowadays the writer about poverty is likely to make much of his own motivations, to assert his involvement, or to agonise over it, even attempting to de-class himself, and always questioning his relatedness because of the strain of trying to relate.

40

Yet once he encountered the poor, his compassion was never tidy or priggish; it was what motivated him to keep on learning and writing. Booth did not attempt to render poverty in its most existential terms. Probably he would have found such efforts contemptible, for he truly believed that between himself and the poor there was an unbridgeable gap of class and culture. But by forcing himself to live among the poor, to make a confrontation with their lives, he achieved a human recognition. His writing is never so opinionated that it does not reflect this.

41

Booth's study of the poor also achieved its first objective: it gave the public some idea of the dimensions and meaning of poverty in London. Never before had the middle classes been told in such harrowing detail about the effects of moral decay and destitution, about the domestic lives of the poor, about the oppression of work, the condition of women workers, the practice of sweating, about the new immigrants.

42

Firstly he found that the proportion in East London was close to thirty-five per cent; that of the 900,000 people in the district, 314,000 were poor; that of these far more than half (185,000) belonged to families earning less than eighteen shillings a week; and that more than half of these in turn (over 100,000) suffered from acute 'distress'.

43

Booth's evidence thus demolished the middle-class myth that poverty resulted from personal failure, vice or improvidence. Despite himself, he implicitly lent support to the argument that poverty was a collective, not an individual, responsibility.

A Booth used this and literally language sparingly. There is a deliberate no-nonsense quality to the prose which may be a trifle off-putting to those accustomed to learning of poverty through the lyricism of a James Agee or the rhetorical indignation of James Baldwin. But, though Booth's primary aim was not to create literature but to describe reality, it is difficult to read his writings today without reflecting on the literary strengths of such a method.

B Instead we feel the simple power of his words even if it never manages to encompass the total reality behind London poverty. What it does manage to convey is strength, resilience, patience, and a certain toughness of observation which seems wholly pertinent to the harsh realities he was called upon to observe. He is hardly ever censorious, never contemptuous and often gently humorous.

C Booth made a second important discovery. On the basis of information received from 4,000 poor people, he concluded that the cause of poverty in about eighty-five per cent of the cases was either 'employment' (both lack of work and low pay) or 'circumstances' (large family and sickness). 'Habit' ('idleness, and thriftlessness') accounted for only about fifteen per cent.

D One of the first to wonder among the habitations of the poor on Chester, Eldon, Ferdinand and Dutton streets, he made empirical descriptions of housing, styles of dress, eating habits, shops and employment, which recall George Orwell's visits nearly fifty years later among the poor of Wigan Pier.

E Politically and administratively, London had scarcely advanced beyond the Middle Ages. In the 1880s with a population of over four million, it still lacked a water, sanitation and public health system; it still suffered from periodic plagues of typhus and cholera; and its poor laws were as archaic and oppressive as ever. There was no central government to speak of. Not until 1888 was a County Council established to assume overall responsibility for education, sewage disposal, housing and hospitals.

F Booth's dry statistical data furnished incontestable proof that previous writers had been in error; they had actually seen only a fraction of London poverty. In the Pall Mall Gazette of 1885, the Social Democratic Federation had contended that twenty-five per cent of the working class was poor, a statistic that Booth had then condemned as shockingly high.

G The result of this is that his writing describes a reality only to be found on the streets of London. As Booth himself pointed out in a letter to his assistant Ernest Aves, 'I am afraid we are sure to shock very many good people in the conclusions – the danger of hurting is rather to be found in the details necessary to support these conclusions. It cannot be entirely avoided, but must never be wanton.'

H Booth's prose shows none of the strains of such an engagement. No doubt he was inspired to begin his researches chiefly because – like many other Englishmen of his class and era – he felt vaguely threatened by the presence of so much poverty and wished to specify the problem in hope of finding the most appropriate solutions to it.

Part 7

You are going to read four extracts related to labour saving devices. For questions **44-53**, choose from the sections **(A-D)**. The sections may be chosen more than once.

Mark your answers **on the separate answer sheet**.

In which section are the following mentioned?

how widespread it was to employ others to do menial domestic duties	**44** ....
how ancient societies dealt with a problem affecting their appearance	**45** ....
the economic effects of two major conflicts	**46** ....
details of the harsh effects of a domestic task	**47** ....
feelings aroused by the ease enjoyed by others who are more affluent	**48** ....
how a workman created something to simplify their job	**49** ....
the possible fatal results of employing a particular device	**50** ....
the conditions that created the mass production of domestic devices	**51** ....
the importance of the weight of a device	**52** ....
the need for an inventor to find an investor	**53** ....

A Men with Ideas

In 1907 James Murray Spangler built a machine for cleaning carpets. The device grew out of his own need, for he was employed as a janitor in a department store and used a broom and carpet sweeper in his daily work. Spangler was apparently familiar with the then new idea of using suction to remove dust and dirt from carpets. It occurred to him that carpets could be more easily cleaned with the sweeping action used in the carpet sweeper.

Using tin and wood as materials and a pillow case for a dust bag, he combined the two ideas in a single machine and although it was a crude and clumsy device, it worked. Spangler lacked the capital, manufacturing capacity and merchandising experience to market his new machine, so he contacted a boyhood friend, William H. Hoover, to try to interest him in the project. Hoover perceived the possibilities of the new device, and a company was formed in 1908 to begin the manufacture of the machine. Three years later, the company started trading under the name of 'Hoover', which remains even today a household word for vacuum cleaners.

B 'State of the Art'

Until the 1920s, domestic servants were common in Europe and any easing of their lot was frowned on. It was not until after the First World War, which drained economies and temporarily obstructed affluent society, that domestic life in Europe started to change. Women were emancipated, domestic labour less easily available and items previously reserved only for the wealthy were now available to all. In America, however, things had been different; the rapidly expanding western frontier had meant hard work and long hours. Combined with high wages and a labour shortage, this had presented a particularly receptive market for mass produced labour saving devices of all kinds.

When the Second World War came, it crippled Europe but left the American economy relatively unscathed, with the result that America took the lead in the production and marketing of household appliances. By the latter part of the century though, the rest of the world had caught up.

C Wrinkles and Creases

For centuries, ironing garments and household linen to free them of wrinkles and creases has been an ever-present chore, and still is even in today's societies where ironed garments continue to be a desired standard.

In the past before ironing boards, irons and ironing machines, the Chinese stretched their garments across bamboo poles as a way of smoothing their garments free of wrinkles. The Greeks folded their garments in chests devised with weights. The Romans used wooden mallets in order to beat garments into smoothness and later invented the first press to serve that purpose. Other devices were undoubtedly used, all of which certainly employed weight or friction as a method of reducing the wrinkles found in fabrics after washing.

In the Middle Ages, it was discovered that cloth pressed while being steamed would hold the shape into which it was moulded. Numerous devices were invented by which heat and pressure could be applied to moistened garments. Iron was the heaviest material available at that time and was a good conductor of heat. Hence the name we still use today.

By the end of the eleventh century. It was recognised that if the irons could be heated from the inside then the labour involved in heating the iron would be reduced. A much later model was heated by gas, and eventually around the 1900s, an iron was developed using an electric current.

D Washing Day

I remember when I was young how laborious washing days were for my mother. In those days we had no running water, and even the simplest handwashing used staggering amounts of time and labour. She used to fill buckets from a communal pump in the village square and haul them back to the house to be heated in a tub over a gas stove. My mother spent what seemed like an eternity on rubbing, wringing and lifting water-laden clothes into a second tub to be rinsed. Large articles like sheets, table cloths and my father's heavy work clothes played havoc with her arms and wrists, and the whole process exposed them to the caustic soap then used.

How my mother would envy those neighbours who were lucky enough to have running water and electricity, not to mention the privileged few who owned what was then known as a clothes washer. She consoled herself with something she'd read somewhere, that this type of washer was a death trap. She might have been right, too; the motor which rotated the tub in the machines was completely unprotected, so water often dripped into it, causing short circuits and jolting shocks. Apart from possibly electrocuting the user, it very often left the clothes in shreds.

Paper 2 – Writing *(1 hour 30 mins)*

Part 1

Read the two texts below.

Write an essay summarising and evaluating the key points from both texts. Use your own words throughout as far as possible, and include your own ideas in your answers.

Write your answer in **240-280 words on the separate answer sheet**.

---

1   **Collaborative Living**

Co-housing is a concept of collaborative housing designed and run by residents who want their own private space but wish to operate as a community. This kind of living emphasises community care and welfare. It relies on a participatory process in which the residents design the community, built on a neighbourhood model: there are private houses or flats for families or individuals but also communal facilities such as lounges, meeting rooms and childcare areas. The organisation is non-hierarchical: different individuals run different activities but there is no overall leader. It is not a commune, however, and operates on a sound financial and legal basis.

New Social Housing

Social housing has finally started to challenge stereotypes and is seeking to restore a human scale and a sense of place to council owned properties. It is typified by contemporary design and energy efficiency within a high-quality environment. The change is social as well as architectural; social housing is no longer segregated off on estates and council houses are dotted in among private homes. On London estates, tenants consulted about new building plans rejected more dense, high-rise designs and voted for less open space but more houses. Tower blocks are being replaced by low rise homes, going back to the old concept of close-knit neighbourhoods.

Write your **essay**.

Part 2

Write an answer to **one** of the questions **2-4** in this part. Write your answer in **280-320** words in an appropriate style **on the separate answer sheet**. Put the question number in the box at the top of the answer sheet.

2 You belong to a group responsible for collecting money to support voluntary organisations such as aid organisations of various kinds. You and your colleagues have collected a large amount of money and distributed it. Write a report saying how the money was collected and which organisations it was given to. Give reasons for your choice

Write your **report**.

3 Your local museum is holding an exhibition entitled *The Way We Used To Live*, depicting scenes and displaying artifacts from the early 19th century. Write an article describing how our lives are different with the modern conveniences we take for granted nowadays and how your life would change without these.

Write your **article**.

4 Recently, you took advantage of a package holiday that was being offered by a well-known tourist agency. The trip was not what you had expected and although you feel that the company was not to blame, you consider that holiday makers need to be aware of potential problems. Write a letter to the newspaper that had advertised the holiday, describing the problems you encountered and saying how these could be dealt with or avoided.

Write your **letter**.

Paper 3 – Listening *(approx. 40 minutes)*

Part 1

You will hear three different extracts. For questions **1-6**, choose the answer (**A, B** or **C**) which fits best according to what you hear. There are two questions for each extract.

Extract One

You hear a woman talking about her humanitarian work in a remote area.

1   The woman decided to work with victims of leprosy because

    A   she was running away from her previous life.

    B   she happened to be in the valley.

    C   she was moved by their plight.

2   People who get the disease often delay treatment

    A   because they think they will be shunned.

    B   because they think leprosy is incurable.

    C   because treatment is too expensive for them.

Extract Two

You hear two people talking about education in a young offender's institution.

3   According to the woman,

    A   education and training is part of the rehabilitation process.

    B   the young people need to be treated more harshly.

    C   the young people do not need to be educated.

4   The man expresses the opinion that

    A   the young people brought misfortune upon themselves.

    B   the young people need to be given a sense of self-esteem.

    C   the young people should be punished more.

Extract Three

You hear an archaeologist being interviewed about Egyptian archaeology.

5   What does the archaeologist say about the existence of the ancient cities up till now?

   A   It was widely believed that they existed.

   B   There was not much concrete proof that they existed.

   C   Some ruins proved that they existed.

6   What does the archaeologist say about the discoveries beneath the sea?

   A   They are well preserved due to their location.

   B   Water pollution has caused them some damage.

   C   It is difficult to remove them without damaging them.

Part 2

You will hear a radio documentary about myths. For questions **7-15**, complete the sentences with a word or short phrase.

Myths were created as a means of explaining [_____ **7** _____] .

Man expressed his feelings about himself and his world in stories with [_____ **8** _____] that we call myths .

The first Greek myths were stories [_____ **9** _____] from parent to child.

Man's fate was controlled by a group of [_____ **10** _____] .

The Greeks used the behaviour of the gods to show them the way to have a [_____ **11** _____] .

The [_____ **12** _____] of the world thought nothing existed beyond the earth.

Because of its ability to give life, Earth was represented as [_____ **13** _____] .

Only later did [_____ **14** _____] gods appear.

Names of mythological figures still familiar today were discovered written on [_____ **15** _____] .

Part 3

You will hear an interview with Margery Paige, a specialist in alternative medicine. For questions **16-20**, choose the answer (**A**, **B**, **C** or **D**) which fits best according to what you hear.

16 Margery tells us that the convention was held because

    A   previous events had been too informal.

    B   more illnesses had come to light in the recent past.

    C   an international meeting was long overdue.

    D   alternative medicine had been slow to catch on among lay people.

17 According to Margery, what was different about this particular event?

    A   It was more widely advertised.

    B   Members of the public were able to attend.

    C   People from opposing schools of thought were welcome.

    D   Medical practitioners were barred.

18 The fact that non-specialists were present meant that

    A   more money was collected in registration fees.

    B   no one could be recognised as being an expert.

    C   the proceedings were more interesting.

    D   clarity became indispensable.

19 The response received by the ideas presented at the convention was

    A   extremely enthusiastic.

    B   rather subdued.

    C   generally favourable.

    D   very sceptical.

20 Margery's conclusion was that the convention had been

    A   an indication of a smaller gap between traditional and alternative views.

    B   a way of improving the professional standing of alternative healers.

    C   an exercise in public relations.

    D   important in strengthening international collaboration.

Part 4

You will hear five short extracts in which different people are talking about how they spend their free time.

Task One

For questions **21-25**, choose from the list (**A-H**), which person each extract relates to. What is the profession of each speaker.

Task Two

For questions **26-30**, choose from the list (**A-H**), the phrase which best summarises what each person feels about their leisure time.

You will hear the recording twice. While you listen, you must complete both tasks.

	Task One				Task Two	
A	doctor			**A**	resentful that work duties intrude into it	
B	office worker					
C	model	Speaker 1	21	**B**	it's limited by tiredness and chores	Speaker 1	26
D	shop owner	Speaker 2	22	**C**	grateful for extended annual holidays	Speaker 2	27
E	medical researcher	Speaker 3	23			Speaker 3	28
F	business executive	Speaker 4	24	**D**	rejuvenated by solitary pursuits	Speaker 4	29
G	sales assistant	Speaker 5	25	**E**	willing to surrender it for business purposes	Speaker 5	30
H	fashion designer			**F**	content to postpone it until established	
				G	determined to use it well	
				H	obliged to spend it with co-workers	

Paper 4 – Speaking *(approx. 16 minutes)*

The speaking test involves two candidates and two examiners. One examiner, the Interlocutor, will speak to you while the other, the Assessor, will just listen.

Part 1 *(2 minutes)*

You will be asked questions in turn about where you live and where you are from, your work, studies and interests, and your views on certain things.

Part 2 *(4 minutes)*

You will be asked to discuss the photographs on page **133** together. There are two stages in this part.

Stage 1
Here are some photographs which show different forms of success. Look at photographs 1 and 3 on page 133 and discuss what difficulties these people might have had to face on their road to success.

Stage 2
Now look at all the pictures. Imagine these photographs are illustrating a lecture on how to achieve success. Discuss how the attitudes of the people shown might lead to their success. Then agree on one new picture showing an example of success that you believe should be included.

Part 3 *(10 minutes)*

You will be asked to talk on your own, comment on what your partner says and join in a three-way discussion with your partner and the Interlocutor around a particular theme.

Change

Candidate A will be asked to look at **prompt card (a)** and talk about it for two minutes.
There are also some ideas on the card to use, if the candidate wishes.

Prompt Card (a)
How important are traditions and continuity in your culture?
– identity – history – local customs

Candidate B will then be given **prompt card (b)** and asked to discuss it for two minutes.
There are also some ideas on the card to use, if the candidate wishes.

Prompt Card (b)
What role do you think technological advances have played in changing society?
– gender roles – information – the family

Candidate B will then be asked a question related to the topic:
• *Do you think traditions are dying out now?*
Then the Interlocutor will invite Candidate A to join in using the following prompt:
• *Do you agree?*

Candidate A will then be asked a question related to the topic:
• *Has technology helped improve relationships?*
Then the Interlocutor will invite Candidate B to join in using the following prompt:
• *What do you think?*

The test will then be concluded with a number of general questions about the topic:
• *To what extent is it important to avoid change?*
• *Do you think that there is a place for tradition in today's ever changing world?*
• *What have been the most significant changes in recent years?*
• *How can one balance cultural values with the challenges of the future?*

Paper 1 – Reading & Use of English (1 hour 30 minutes)

Part 1

For questions **1-8**, read the text below and decide which answer (**A, B, C** or **D**) best fits each gap. Mark your answers **on the separate answer sheet**.

There is an example at the beginning (**0**).

0   **A**   contrast   **B**   diversity   **C**   difference   **D**   variance

0	A	B	C	D
	☐	☐	▣	☐

Hi Tech Cricket

The Hawk-eye system has made a great deal of **(0)** .....C..... to the sports of tennis and cricket in recent years. The system, which is a good example of how military technology can be used for peaceful **(1)** .... , is based on missile tracking technology. The system works by placing high speed cameras at different locations and angles around the cricket **(2)** .... or area of play and using the data provided by the cameras to analyse the trajectory of a ball to help cricket and tennis umpires make accurate decisions. It is especially useful for such difficult decisions as LBW in cricket (leg before wicket) when the umpire must **(3)** .... whether the ball would have hit the stumps had the batsman's leg not got in the way. Modern bowlers **(4)** .... the ball at such incredible speeds that umpires can have difficulty in following the ball with the **(5)** .... eye.

The software in the system can predict **(6)** .... an accuracy of 5mm the direction of a ball and at the same time **(7)** .... statistical data on the height the ball and the speed it travelled at. This means that **(8)** .... disputed decisions in tennis and cricket can be definitively settled.

1	**A**	reasons	**B**	plans	**C**	ideas	**D**	purposes
2	**A**	court	**B**	field	**C**	park	**D**	rink
3	**A**	determine	**B**	describe	**C**	infer	**D**	evaluate
4	**A**	convey	**B**	send	**C**	deliver	**D**	conduct
5	**A**	exposed	**B**	naked	**C**	bare	**D**	uncovered
6	**A**	at	**B**	from	**C**	with	**D**	by
7	**A**	stockpile	**B**	hoard	**C**	converge	**D**	collect
8	**A**	blazingly	**B**	fiercely	**C**	wildly	**D**	brutally

Part 2

For questions **9-16**, read the text below and think of the word which best fits each space. Use only **one** word in each space. There is an example at the beginning (**0**). Write your answers **IN CAPITAL LETTERS on the separate answer sheet**.

Example: | 0 | S | U | C | H | | | | | | | | | | | | | |

The Seasons

Measuring the seasons by ordinary natural events, (**0**) ....SUCH..... as the departure of migrating birds (**9**) .... the appearance of the first flowers, shows that spring now occurs ten to thirty days earlier than it did and autumn is also arriving later.

Traditional data on phenology – the study of the timing of natural events – goes (**10**) .... to 1736 in Britain. Taken (**11**) .... isolation, phenological data may not mean (**12**) ...., but the received wisdom from ecology is about interconnectedness. Higher temperatures which delay the onset of winter often provide animals with misleading cues. (**13**) ...., some species will breed later and then find that their food source has been destroyed (**14**) .... winter finally arrives. Competition for winter food will probably increase too, as birds stop migrating south in winter, as has (**15**) .... happened in a (**16**) .... of cases.

Part 3

For questions **17-24**, read the text below. Use the word given in capitals at the end of some of the lines to form a word that fits in the space in the same line. There is an example at the beginning (**0**). Write your answers **IN CAPITAL LETTERS on the separate answer sheet.**

Example: | **0** | B | R | U | T | A | L | | | | | | | | | | |

Hiking in the Countryside

Winter in the British countryside can be very **(0)** ....BRUTAL....... but it has   **BRUTE**

such **(17)** .... beauty that for many people   **BREATH**

(18) .... the pleasure of long country walks is out of the   **FORE**

question, however severe the weather.

Fortunately, there is a very wide range of hiking gear from which to choose,

from the traditional waxed jackets to modern Gore-tex clothing and

footwear. But, **(19)** .... of your clothing preferences, of all   **RESPECT**

your **(20)** .... , the main one should be to keep warm and   **PRIOR**

dry. Layering clothing is a good idea. Start with thermal underwear topped

with an outer shell of jackets and overtrousers in **(21)** ....   **PERMEATE**

fabrics that keep out the wind and rain but don't make you sweat. Even in

wet weather, rubber boots are unsuitable for proper long walks. You will

need good boots with ankle support and good **(22)** .... A   **TRACT**

small rucksack of around 20-litre capacity is fine for short walks but the

intrepid hiker will need a **(23)** .... larger one of up to 40   **SUBSTANCE**

litres. Hikers' rucksacks have been considerably **(24)** .... in   **LIGHT**

recent years as more and more lightweight fabrics have been developed.

Part 4

For questions **25-30**, complete the second sentence so that it has a similar meaning to the first sentence, using the word given. **Do not change the word given.** You must use between **three** and **eight** words, including the word given. Here is an example (**0**).

Example:

0   We are able to afford a holiday, because I was promoted.

result

As .... , we are able to afford a holiday.

0	*a result of my promotion*

Write **only** the missing words **on the separate answer sheet.**

---

25   When neither side accepted the proposals to solve the crisis, negotiations collapsed.

proposed

The failure of .... to
the crisis meant negotiations collapsed.

26   My dog hurt itself when it tried to jump the fence.

due

My dog's .... to jump the fence.

27   The new motorway will involve demolishing a lot of old houses.

way

A lot of old houses .... for the new motorway.

28   If you remember, I was the one who started this project in 1995.

cast

If ...., I was the one who started this project in 1995.

29   He protested that he had always kept his promises to me.

gone

He protested that .... to me.

30   A contract between the two parties was drawn up by a local solicitor.

responsible

A local solicitor .... the two parties.

Part 5

You are going to read part of the introduction to a book of Welsh short stories. For questions **31-36**, choose the answer (**A, B, C** or **D**) which you think fits best according to the text. Mark your answers **on the separate answer sheet**.

Welsh Stories

It was an American wit who listed one of man's greatest virtues as the art of making the long story short, but he was saying nothing about the short story, which has its own necessary length, neither too long nor too short, and is at its best when it presents a revealing insight into a person in a particular situation. What interests me most is being at the core of another life, seeing new light thrown upon it through the mind and world of the central character. It is a help if I am so involved at the outset that my attention does not wander and that my sympathies are immediately engaged, but ultimately, I must know more at the end than I did at the beginning. Now and again, let it also be stated, I can certainly do with a smile. These stories have been chosen to fulfil such requirements where they can be met, but they are in addition, of a place and a time. The place is Wales and the time is the twentieth century, since the short story is a comparatively new arrival here. They reflect Wales, not always flatteringly, as it is and has been. English writers, it has been said, are often refugees from society, but almost all the stories in this book written by Welsh men and women show a concern for a particular landscape or community. It is as if Welsh writers cannot escape this involvement, and often there is also a sense of characters off stage, present but unseen at the storyteller's elbow. Perhaps the reason for this awareness of others is that so many of us have lived in crowded places, and, while it is not always healthy, it is a part of the Welsh experience which is very different from that of our neighbours.

I have not otherwise been able to define a specific characteristic of the Welsh story which makes it immediately identifiable, save for the nationality or place of residence of the writer, but it should be pointed out that some Welsh writers writing in English have faced particular difficulties when they have felt the need to emphasise their difference from English counterparts. Often this need has led to stereotyped patterns of speech, the whimsicality of which often gives a false impression. At the back of it, one suspects the seductive pressures of those who like to see their Welshmen as clowns or 'characters', but it should also be said that many Welshmen have woven myths about themselves and their country with mischievous delight, and one doubts if they needed much encouragement. Of course, this forced use of language can be detected in other literatures, some of them colonialist, and it is perhaps the inevitable consequence of the dominance of a distant metropolis. Having said that, it is only fair to note that many of the short story writers who write in English received their first encouragement in England, and indeed some of them, like Alun Lewis, represented here by an almost unknown story of army life, are at their best away from home. In his case, he was probably more searching as an observer with a foreign eye and his stories dealing with English life were perhaps more acutely observed than those dealing with his native South Wales. There is an abundance of riches from which the anthologist may choose and my task has been made easier by the selections of other editors whose choices I have tried not to duplicate where possible.

I have said that these stories were chosen because they please one reader and are of a place and time, but I have also had a number of other considerations in mind and I have tried to represent all Welsh writers, including those whose work belies the concept of Wales as a homogeneous society, some who write in English and others who write exclusively in Welsh and for whom Welsh is the first language. All arguments about degrees of Welshness I find to be fruitless; for me, the story is the thing, although on re-reading so many stories in preparing this volume, I could not help but detect the security of so many writers in the Welsh language, which has freed them from painful attempts to emphasise their nationality, a strain which affected the work of their counterparts writing in English for a time. Ironically, this freedom seems to be in danger of ending and, judging by some of the stories made available in translation, appears to have been replaced by the aim of political conversion, to the detriment, in my view, of the storyteller's art. However, the representation of writers in the Welsh language, translated here, is varied enough to warrant a further anthology comprised solely of stories translated from the original. It is my hope that the Wales of the past and the present is well represented in this volume, together with the world of work and workmen in some of our more ravaged terrains, an aspect which has tended to be neglected in the past.

31 What does the writer say is essential when he reads a short story?

    A   It should be the correct length for a short story.

    B   The story should be an amusing one.

    C   It should deepen his understanding of human nature.

    D   It should hold his attention from the start.

32 The writer says the stories show

    A   how English writers resort to escapism.

    B   real life in Wales in the past and in the present.

    C   a new form of writing.

    D   the best aspects of Welsh life.

33 The writer suggests that, unlike English writers, Welsh writers

    A   have a strong sense of place.

    B   become closely involved with the characters they write about.

    C   only write about densely populated areas.

    D   avoid writing about specific people or places.

34 What does the writer say helped him choose the stories in the book?

    A   He could initially ignore a number of stories.

    B   There were a large number of Welsh stories to choose from.

    C   Many writers lived outside Wales.

    D   Their popularity with the reading public guided him.

35 The stories in the book

    A   are all translations from the original Welsh language.

    B   put across the idea that all Welsh people are the same.

    C   represent a wide variety of Welsh authors.

    D   have a tendency to accentuate the author's origins.

36 What does the writer say about the writers who write in Welsh today?

    A   They represent Wales throughout its history.

    B   Writing a good story may not be their main purpose.

    C   They have less skill than writers using English.

    D   The translations of their work are not always accurate.

Part 6

You are going to read an extract from a short story. Seven paragraphs have been removed from the extract. Choose from the paragraphs **A-H** the one which fits each gap (**37-43**). There is one extra paragraph which you do not need to use. **Mark your answers on the separate answer sheet**.

The Editor

Jack Mulholland folded the paper and rubbed at the tension knotting his brow. It was going to be a difficult morning. He picked up the phone. 'Ask Roz Moore and Gaby in, will you.' He tried not to sound terse.

37

This was enough to set the eruption off. Mulholland's face contorted in rage. 'In all my years as editor of this august publication, I have never seen such an execrable column.' he bellowed, 'Who allowed it? You have deeply offended the vast majority of our core readership!'

38

Mulholland's eyes narrowed and his jaw became rigid. 'Is there any point in asking why you didn't refer the offending article to your senior editor?' Gaby shrank in horror and Roz's heart sank.

39

'Well, no, but I really don't think it will come to that,' Roz said, trying to sound authoritative, 'Let's get another columnist to write a reply and make sure we publish a few readers' letters. We could turn this to our advantage,' she said in as light a tone as she could muster.

40

'If you don't think that will work then you'll have to take her on yourself, Jack.' Roz's own temper was beginning to fray. Gaby knew now was not the time to offer any kind of advice and stood looking at her feet.

41

She started to sob. 'My media career is over before it even began!' she wailed. Roz gave her a stern look. 'He'll have a good fight with Liz and then he'll do what I suggested in the first place. Just stay out of his way for a few days and he'll have completely forgotten about it'.

42

Roz slammed the door of her office and slumped in the chair at her desk. Jack Mulholland was one of the finest editors in the country and a man she'd long admired for his tenacity in a cutthroat business. But perhaps he was, finally, beginning to lose his edge.

43

Before she had a chance to give him a piece of her mind, he told her that Liz herself would write an apologetic article. He said she'd not been too pleased with the idea, but he'd charmed her into it. Now he worked his charm on Roz. 'Lunch? My treat.' 'Alright, but if you ever dress me down in front of a junior like that again it will cost you more than lunch.'

A Gaby stood frozen to the spot, tears springing to her eyes. Roz's mind raced in a desperate search for a method of damage limitation. But before she could come up with anything, Gaby had started to blab. 'What could I do to stop her? She's our star columnist. She insisted it go up or I'd rue the day.'

B 'If someone had come to me in the first place, I wouldn't have to deal with the imperious she-devil now, would I,' he thundered. 'Get out my sight, the pair of you.' Roz considered saying something but guided a dazed Gaby out of the room instead.

C 'So you want to set another columnist head to head with Liz Green, as a containment plan? You know she won't stand for it and the next thing she'll do is defect to one of our competitors, who would be only too happy to have her and the other half of our readership she'd take with her!'

D A few moments later, a senior editor and one of her team walked into his office. Roz, an old hand on Fleet street, picked up the warning signs emanating from her editor's eyes on her antennae. Jack Mulholland was a formidable man, with a short reign on a volcanic temper. Gaby, too inexperienced to recognise the danger signals, breezed into the office with an air of cultured confidence.

E The world of journalism was moving on and Mulholland wasn't moving quite as fast. He still clung to the comforting old ways. She wasn't going to let him have the complete upper hand, though. For one thing, he'd humiliated her in front of her subordinate. She phoned him.

F She had no idea what she was going to do to salvage the situation. Should she phone him or let him stew for a while. He was usually much easier to manipulate when he'd calmed down. She would plan her attack.

G Roz took the plunge. 'Gaby called me to ask for advice on the piece. I told her controversy is good. It ups sales, so let it ride.' She tried to keep level eye contact with Mulholland. His eyes were cold and rock steady. 'Is one issue's sales increase worth losing half our readership over?' he asked with undisguised sarcasm.

H Relief flooded Gaby's face. 'Are you sure?' But Roz was already marching back to her office in long, purposeful strides. Gaby took this as a sign to make herself scarce and headed for the door. Her hands were still shaking and the calming atmosphere of *The Criterion* beckoned.

Part 7

You are going to read extracts about food and cooking. For questions **44-53**, choose from the sentences (**A-D**). The texts may be chosen more than once.

Mark your answers **on the separate answer sheet**.

In which section are the following mentioned?

a group of foods that changed the way an area of the world cooked	**44** ....
a period of time when access to food was restricted	**45** ....
a comparison of the process of producing a substance with that used for some other foods, too	**46** ....
the global popularity of a particular food	**47** ....
an interest in discovering more about unfamiliar types of food	**48** ....
the discrepancy between the amount of a type of food produced and the demand for it	**49** ....
a substance that reinforces the savoury aspect of food	**50** ....
a way of determining the strength of a foodstuff	**51** ....
using literary forms to talk about food dishes	**52** ....
worries about the ethical future of a food industry	**53** ....

A Monosodium Glutamate

Good food is one of life's pleasures and even 1,200 years ago, oriental cooks knew that food tasted better when prepared with a soup stock made from a type of seaweed. But it was only in 1908 that Japanese scientists identified the ingredient responsible for enhancing flavour.

That ingredient is known today by its scientific name, monosodium glutamate. It is often referred to as MSG and it is an amino acid found in virtually all foods. The bound form is linked to other amino acids in proteins and is manufactured in the human body. The free form of glutamate in foods enhances food flavours. Tomatoes, cheese and mushrooms are just some free glutamate rich foods. Free glutamate content increases during ripening, bringing out a fuller taste in many foods and is made as a flavour enhancer by a fermentation process similar to that used for making soy sauce and vinegar.

People have long known about the four basic tastes - sweet, sour, salty and bitter. But now a fifth basic taste called umami has been recognised. This is imparted to foods by glutamate and is responsible for the savoury taste of many foods, such as tomatoes and cheese.

B Organic Food & Business!

Organic farmers pride themselves on fostering sustainable agriculture, but it remains to be seen if the industry's rapid growth is in fact sustainable.

One challenge facing the industry is to bring the price of organic products more in line with those of conventional products. The price of organic ingredients is improving but demand still outpaces supply. However, supply issues are overshadowed by the fact that the organic foods sector continues to grow faster than the food industry as a whole, fundamentally due to the natural alliance between organic crops and processed foods. Firstly, organic foods earmarked for processing do not have to be as cosmetically perfect as their fresh counterparts. In addition, freezing or tinning reduces many of the shelf-life problems associated with fresh produce. It was only a question of time before mainstream food companies woke up to these synergies.

The pioneers of the organic food industry view the growing presence of major food companies in their markets as a mixed blessing. Many smaller companies fear that the ideals of organic agriculture will be compromised. Others think major food companies will help persuade consumers to buy organic products through the power of their branding.

C Chilli

Capsicums, commonly known as chillis, come in all dimensions and colours from the tiny, pointed, extremely hot, bird's eye chilli, to the large, mild, fleshy peppers like the Anaheim. Indigenous to Central and South America and the West Indies, they were cultivated long before the Spanish conquest, which was the eventual cause of their introduction to Europe. Chillis along with tomatoes, avocados, vanilla and chocolate changed the flavours of the known world. Today, there are around 400 different varieties of chillis grown. They are easy to cultivate and are one of the world's most widely distributed crops, available for sale at most food outlets.

In 1902, a method was developed for measuring the strength of a given variety of capsicum, ranking it on a predetermined scale. This originally meant tasting the peppers, but nowadays it can be done more accurately with the help of computers to rate the peppers in units to indicate parts per million of capsaicin. This potent chemical not only causes the fiery sensation, but also triggers the brain to produce endorphins, natural painkillers that promote a sense of well-being.

D Writing about Cooking

Two cookery writers are often credited with the present revival of interest in food and cooking. Elizabeth David discovered her taste for good food when she lived with a French family for two years. After returning to England she learnt to cook so that she could reproduce some of the food that she had come to appreciate in France. Her first book appeared when rationing was still in force after the war and most of the ingredients she had so lovingly described were not available. At the time her book was read rather than used, and it created a yearning for good ingredients and for a way of life that saw more in food than mere sustenance. Her later books confirmed her position as the most inspirational and influential cookery writer in the English language. She shared with Jane Grigson an absorbing interest in the literature of cookery.

Jane Grigson was brought up in the north-east of England, where there is a strong tradition of good eating, but it was not until she began to spend time in France that she became really interested in food. She was renowned for her fine writing on food and cookery, often catching the imagination with a deftly chosen fragment of history or poetry, but never failing to explain the 'why' as well as the 'how' of cookery.

Paper 2 – Writing *(1 hour 30 mins)*

Part 1

Read the two texts below.

Write an essay summarising and evaluating the key points from both texts. Use your own words throughout as far as possible, and include your own ideas in your answers.

Write your answer in **240-280 words on the separate answer sheet**.

1 ### Extremely Dangerous, Extremely Reckless

The past few decades have seen a massive rise in the number of people participating in extreme sports, many of which are extremely dangerous, not only to participants but, in some cases, to bystanders too. The question remains as to whether there should be more restrictions on these sports because of the cost of rescuing people from dangerous situations and for treating injuries sustained while taking part in these sports. The drain on common resources caused by thrill seekers taking ridiculous risks is unacceptable.

Keeping Things in Perspective

There is no doubt that many extreme sports can be dangerous. However, this has been over-hyped in the media. Firstly, all sports have an element of danger to them and treatment of injuries from jogging and playing tennis cost the health service more than the low number of injuries caused by extreme sports, simply because they are still minority activities with few participants. To put it into perspective, a handful of people are killed every year taking part in extreme sports, while thousands are killed in road accidents, yet no one is calling for cars to be banned.

Write your **essay**.

Part 2

Write an answer to **one** of the questions **2-4** in this part. Write your answer in **280-320** words in an appropriate style **on the separate answer sheet**. Put the question number in the box at the top of the answer sheet.

2   You are a member of a town planning committee. You have done some research on what to do with a disused factory site in your town. The options include:
   – turning the site into a park.
   – using the site as an adventure playground.
   – renovating the building and converting it to small workshops for rent.
   Write a report about the advantages and disadvantages of each option and recommend the option that would be most suitable.

   Write your **report**.

3   A magazine has asked its readers to exchange information about the kind of films and books they like most and least. Write a review of two books you have read, or two films you have seen, giving reasons why the one appeals to you and the other does not.

   Write your **review**.

4   There has been a proposal that a zoo and an aquarium should be established in your town or city and a large area of land has been set aside for this purpose. Regular shows for the public have been suggested as a means of funding these, with some of the animals, such as seals, dolphins and tigers, being trained to take part. A local newspaper has invited readers to contribute articles on their experiences of zoos and aquariums and their views on animals being used for entertainment.

   Write your **article**.

Part 1

You will hear three different extracts. For questions **1-6**, choose the answer (**A, B** or **C**) which fits best according to what you hear. There are two questions for each extract.

Extract One

You hear a discussion on a book about film directors.

1   What conclusion about success does the book suggest?

    A   Talent is enough to secure a directing job.

    B   Most directors lack the necessary dedication.

    C   Directors run into difficulties along the way.

2   It is implied that directors are

    A   arrogant.

    B   dependent.

    C   creative.

Extract Two

You hear a traveller talking about an encounter with a tortoise.

3   The speaker values the turns in the road because they

    A   make the journey enjoyable.

    B   are full of interesting surprises.

    C   warrant cautious driving.

4   Why does the speaker compare the appearance of the tortoise to a privilege?

    A   It was unexpected.

    B   It was touching.

    C   It was rare.

Extract Three

You hear a report about a recent trend in middle-aged men.

5   To what does the speaker attribute the increase in sales of expensive racing bikes?

   A   The desire to stay fit

   B   The achievements of athletes

   C   The marketing strategies of retailers

6   What advice does the speaker have for wives of men who have bought an expensive bike?

   A   Remember that it could have been worse.

   B   Buy yourself a sports car.

   C   Make sure that your teenage children are allowed to use it.

Part 2

You will hear a report on how English has become a global language. For questions **7-15**, complete the sentences with a word or short phrase.

The two most usual kinds of migraine are known as [**7**] migraine.

The moment the signs of an approaching migraine appear [**8**] should be used.

Headaches are not the only indication of migraine; these are very often preceded by [**9**].

The speaker feels [**10**] during an attack and has problems

expressing herself clearly.

The signs that indicate migraine may make people think you are having a [**11**].

It is an upsetting and [**12**] experience.

A variety of things can [**13**] a migraine.

Slump migraine can occur when a source of anxiety is [**14**].

The speaker's attacks are less [**15**] now than before.

Part 3

You will hear an interview with Dr Timothy Cowey, a prominent palaeontologist, who is discussing a forthcoming expedition. For questions **16-20**, choose the answer (**A, B, C** or **D**) which fits best according to what you hear.

16 Which of the following facts about the Gobi Desert is false?

   A   The desert is located in Mongolia.

   B   Many mines can be found there.

   C   It contains areas rich in fossils.

   D   It is home to the Nemegat Basin.

17 When are 'The Flaming Cliffs' at their most beautiful?

   A   During the night.

   B   In the light of the rising sun.

   C   Anytime during the day.

   D   When they catch the setting sun.

18 According to Dr Cowey,

   A   there are more dinosaur eggs to be found.

   B   there is nothing more to be learnt about birds.

   C   animals developed flight to survive.

   D   fossils show birds in flight.

19 The excavation

   A   is not restricted to experts.

   B   is only for professionals.

   C   is the best in the world.

   D   is difficult to find.

20 Hongoryn Els

   A   was the site of one previous excavation.

   B   is close to the sea.

   C   is a potentially valuable site.

   D   is of no particular interest.

Part 4

You will hear five short extracts in which teachers talk about their job.

Task One
For questions **21-25**, choose from the list (**A-H**), what aspect of their job each teacher particularly enjoys.

Task Two
For questions **26-30**, choose from the list (**A-H**), what negative aspect of their job each teacher mentions.

You will hear the recording twice. While you listen, you must complete both tasks.

A	the opportunity to keep learning		
B	the chance to encourage talent	Speaker 1	21
C	working with young people	Speaker 2	22
		Speaker 3	23
D	encouraging disadvantaged youths	Speaker 4	24
E	its compatability with family life	Speaker 5	25
F	helping students achieve their goals		
G	the long holidays		
H	interacting with diverse people		

A	uninterested students		
B	repetitive classwork teaching	Speaker 1	26
C	the constraints of testing techniques	Speaker 2	27
D	comparatively low pay	Speaker 3	28
E	unrealistic patental expectations	Speaker 4	29
		Speaker 5	30
F	the heavy workload		
G	discipline problems		
H	the lack of support from some parents		

Paper 4 – Speaking *(approx. 16 minutes)*

The speaking test involves two candidates and two examiners. One examiner, the Interlocutor, will speak to you while the other, the Assessor, will just listen.

Part 1 *(2 minutes)*

You will be asked questions in turn about where you live and where you are from, your work, studies and interests, and your views on certain things.

Part 2 *(4 minutes)*

You will be asked to discuss the photographs on page **134** together. There are two stages in this part.

Stage 1
Here are some photographs which show different forms of stress. Look at photographs 1 and 3 on page 134 and discuss to what degree you would find these situations stressful.

Stage 2
Now look at all the pictures. You are giving a talk concerning the effects of stress on our everyday lives. Discuss why each of these situations is stressful and then decide on the picture to use in your talk, which best illustrates stress in everyday life.

Part 3 *(10 minutes)*

You will be asked to talk on your own, comment on what your partner says and join in a three-way discussion with your partner and the Interlocutor around a particular theme.

Education

Candidate A will be asked to look at **prompt card (a)** and talk about it for two minutes.
There are also some ideas on the card to use, if the candidate wishes.

Prompt Card (a)
What have been some of the greatest influences on your educational choices?
– family – friends – job prospects

Candidate B will then be asked a question related to the topic:
● *What role do teachers play in educational choices?*
Then the Interlocutor will invite Candidate A to join in using the following prompt:
● *Do you agree?*

Candidate B will then be given **prompt card (b)** and asked to discuss it for two minutes.
There are also some ideas on the card to use, if the candidate wishes.

Prompt Card (b)
How do you think being educated at home by parents, as opposed to being sent to a traditional school, would affect a child?
– qualifications – socialisation – academic achievement

Candidate A will then be asked a question related to the topic:
● *What advantages do you think there are to home tutoring?*
Then the Interlocutor will invite Candidate B to join in using the following prompt:
● *What do you think?*

The test will then be concluded with a number of general questions about the topic:

● *In what ways do you think school facilities can be improved?*
● *Do you think that schools should be accountable for the fact that children fail to learn?*
● *What kind of subjects should be compulsory?*
● *Should schools offer a general education or concentrate on preparing children for a career?*

CPE Practice Tests ②

Visual Material for the Speaking Paper

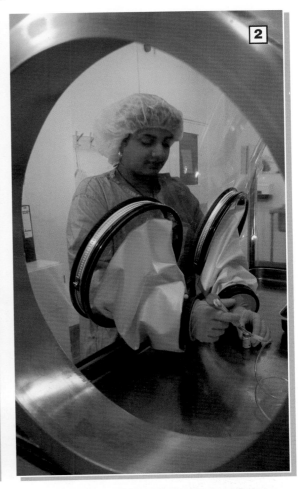

Self-expression

Part 2

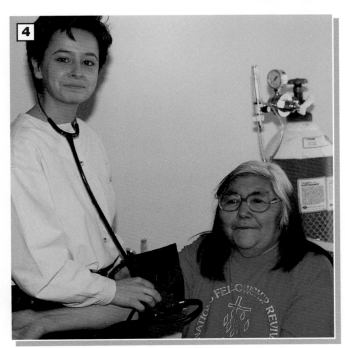

Stress in our everyday lives